NATIONS
OF THE WORLD
INDIA

Anita Dalal

RAINTREE
STECK-VAUGHN
PUBLISHERS

A Harcourt Company

Austin   New York
www.steck-vaughn.com

Steck-Vaughn Company

First published 2002 by Raintree Steck-Vaughn Publishers,
an imprint of Steck-Vaughn Company.
Copyright © 2002 Brown Partworks Limited.

Library of Congress Cataloging-in-Publication Data

Dalal, Anita
India / Anita Dalal.
p. cm -- (Nations of the world)
Includes bibliographical references and index.
ISBN 0-7398-1289-0
1. India--Juvenile literature. [1. India] I. Title. II. Nations of the world (Austin, Tex.)

DS407.D3 2001
954--dc21

00–068858
CIP

Printed and bound in the United States
1 2 3 4 5 6 7 8 9 0   05 04 03 02 01

Brown Partworks Limited
Project Editor: Peter Jones
Designer: Joan Curtis
Cartographer: William Le Bihan
Picture Researcher: Liz Clachan
Editorial Assistant: Anthony Shaw
Indexer: Kay Ollerenshaw

Raintree Steck-Vaughn
Publishing Director: Walter Kossmann
Art Director: Richard Johnson
Editor: Frank Tarsitano

Front cover: The Taj Mahal (background); crouching tiger (left); Asoka Pillar (top left)
Title page: The Red Fort, Delhi.

The acknowledgments on p. 128 form part of this copyright page.

Contents

Foreword

Since ancient times, people have gathered together in communities where they could share and trade resources and strive to build a safe and happy environment. Gradually, as populations grew and societies became more complex, communities expanded to become nations—groups of people who felt sufficiently bound by a common heritage to work together for a shared future.

Land has usually played an important role in defining a nation. People have a natural affection for the landscape in which they grew up. They are proud of its natural beauties—the mountains, rivers, and forests—and of the towns and cities that flourish there. People are proud, too, of their nation's history—the shared struggles and achievements that have shaped the way they live today.

Religion, culture, race, and lifestyle, too, have sometimes played a role in fostering a nation's identity. Often, though, a nation includes people of different races, beliefs, and customs. Many may have come from distant countries. Nations have rarely been fixed, unchanging things, either territorially or racially. Throughout history, borders have changed, often under the pressure of war, and people have migrated across the globe in search of a new life or because they are fleeing from oppression or disaster. The world's nations are still changing today: Some nations are breaking up and new nations are forming.

Indian civilization is one of the oldest in the world, and first formed around the banks of the Indus River over 4,000 years ago. It was in India that two of the world's major religions, Hinduism and Buddhism, emerged. Although protected by the towering Himalaya Mountains to the north, the subcontinent's fertile river plains and thriving agriculture attracted invaders. India's southern coasts played a major part in medieval trade with China and Europe and from the 18th century until independence in 1947, it was ruled by the British. Recently the country has worked hard to overcome problems of poverty and underdevelopment, while maintaining the incredible richness of its cultural traditions.

Introduction

INDIA

India is one of the world's most colorful, exciting, and varied places. The country's history stretches back thousands of years. It has an economy based on the latest modern technology as well as centuries-old farming methods; and India is home to a multitude of different religions and languages. In 1897 the American writer Mark Twain (1835–1910) described India as: "the land of dreams and romance, of fabulous wealth and fabulous poverty, of splendor and rags, of palaces and hovels, of famine and pestilence, of genies and giants and Aladdin lamps, of tigers and elephants, the cobra and the jungle, the country of a hundred nations and a hundred tongues, of a thousand religions and two million gods…" Twain's description is still accurate today.

Walk down any busy street in the country's capital, Delhi, and you will see a business executive talking on her mobile phone, while a holy man, dressed in yellow robes, sits on the sidewalk receiving alms. Poor dwellings exist next door to luxury high-rise apartments. It is possible to travel from the wettest city in the world to some of the world's driest deserts—and still be in India.

India lies in southern Asia and most of the country is surrounded by ocean: the Arabian Sea, to the west, the Bay of Bengal, to the east, and the Indian Ocean, to the south. The country's northern border is formed by the highest mountain range in the world, the Himalayas.

Jodhpur in Rajasthan in northeast India is often called the Blue City.

Blue was traditionally the color of the houses of Brahmins, or holy men.

FACT FILE

- India is the world's most populous democracy.

- India has the second-largest population in the world and is projected to overtake China by 2030.

- India is home to two of the world's major religions—Hinduism and Buddhism.

- Indians call their country *Bharat Mata* ("Mother India").

- Hindi is the third-most spoken language in the world after Mandarin Chinese and English.

- The cost of living in India is 40 percent of that in the United States.

Known as the "tricolor," India's flag is made up of three equal horizontal bands of color. The top band is saffron, representing Hinduism, the green band represents Islam, and the central white band represents all other religions.

The rupee comes in 500, 100, 50, 20, 10, 5, 2, and 1 notes, but the 5, 2, and 1 notes are being phased out.

MOTHER INDIA

Modern-day India's size and boundaries date from 1947, when the country gained independence from Great Britain. The country's administrative regions are the result of historical divisions between different religions, and of the different princely states that existed before independence (*see* p. 59). The centuries' old conflict between the members of two religions, Hinduism and Islam, has dominated much of India's history. At the beginning of the 21st century, India and its Muslim neighbor, Pakistan, continue to argue over the future of the northern state of Kashmir (*see* p. 16), which both countries claim as their own.

India is a federal republic made up of 28 states and seven union territories. It is a democracy—that is, its government is elected by the people. In practice, however, one political party, the Congress Party, was the major party in government from 1947 until the elections of 1996, when the Hindu nationalist party, the BJP, became the largest party represented in the government.

India's tricolor flag has a 24-spoke wheel (*chakra*) in the center white band. The *chakra* is a symbol taken from the reign of India's first great emperor, Asoka, who became ruler of India in 272 B.C. (*see* p. 48). The design of the wheel is based on the Asokan pillar at Sarnath, the city where the founder of the Buddhist religion, the Buddha (*see* p. 114), first preached. Before 1947, India was part of the British empire, and the tricolor flag was created to symbolize an independent India.

The currency of India is the rupee. On the back of the rupee notes, the value of the note is written in India's official languages (*see* opposite)—Marathi and the ancient written language of Sanskrit are missing from the list.

The National Anthem

The words of India's national anthem were written by the Nobel Prize-winning author Rabindranath Tagore and were first sung on December 27, 1911. The song was adopted as the national anthem for the newly independent India on January 24, 1950. Before that date, the Indian anthem had been "I Bow to the Motherland" ("*Vanda Mataran*"), which was sung at Indian Congress Party meetings during India's fight for independence from Britain (*see* pp. 66–67). But India's first prime minister after independence, Jawaharlal Nehru, felt the old anthem was inappropriate. Only the first verse of the five-verse song is used in the current national anthem. Tagore translated the song into English himself.

"*Jana Gana Mana*"
*Thou art the ruler of the minds of all
   people, dispenser of India's destiny.
Thy name rouses the hearts of Punjab,
   Sind, Gujarat, and Maratha,
Of the Dravida and Orissa and Bengal;
It echoes in the hills of Vindhyas and
   Himalaya,
Mingles in the music of Yamuna and
   Ganges,
And is chanted by the waves of the
   Indian Sea.
They pray for thy blessings and sing thy
   praise.
The saving of all people waits in thy
   hand,
Thou dispenser of India's destiny,
Victory, victory, victory to thee.*

LANGUAGES AND PEOPLE

The national language of India is Hindi, which is the first language of 30 percent of the population, most of whom live in the north. There are 16 other official languages each with its own script, most of these are spoken in specific regions. For example, in the eastern state of Bengal, Bengali is the main language. Apart from Hindi, India's other official languages are: Assamese, Bengali, Gujarati, Kannada, Kashmiri, Konkani, Malayalam, Marathi, Nepali, Oriya, Punjabi, Sanskrit, Sindhi, Tamil, Telugu, and Urdu.

In addition to the official languages, there are more than 1,000 other languages and dialects. (A dialect is a variation of a language.) India is one of the few countries in the world where two of its citizens might not be able to understand each other's language.

Modern English has borrowed many words from the languages of the Indian subcontinent, including dungarees, khaki, pajamas, sandals, shampoo, and verandah.

India is still largely a rural country. Although poverty exists in both urban and rural communities, the villages in rural India provide a better system of support than the crowded shanties of India's cities.

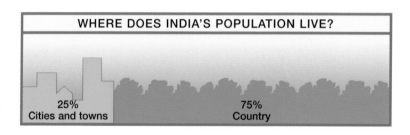

WHERE DOES INDIA'S POPULATION LIVE?

25%
Cities and towns

75%
Country

English was brought to India by the British rulers, and for many years, it was the language that all educated Indians spoke. Today, English continues to be the most important language for business and international communication and is the official language of the legal profession. The Indian government's attempts to replace English with Hindi in schools, universities, and offices have failed because the languages of south India bear little relation to Hindi, and southern Indians prefer to speak English rather than Hindi. Throughout India, middle-class parents prefer their children to learn English, as well as their regional language, because they believe learning English will help the children in their future careers. Indian English is often nicknamed "Hinglish" because it is English with a peculiarly Indian choice of words. To catch a criminal in Hinglish, for instance, is to "nab a miscreant."

The Indian population originates from two main ethnic groups: Indo-Aryan and Dravidian. The Dravidians are the original inhabitants of India, while the Indo-Aryans invaded India around 1500 B.C. pushing the Dravidians south (*see* p. 45).

India has the second-largest population in the world after China. Its population rose rapidly in the second half of the 20th century. In 1947, at the time of Indian independence, the population was over 300 million.

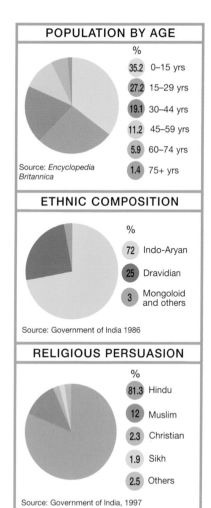

POPULATION BY AGE

%

35.2 0–15 yrs
27.2 15–29 yrs
19.1 30–44 yrs
11.2 45–59 yrs
5.9 60–74 yrs
1.4 75+ yrs

Source: *Encyclopedia Britannica*

ETHNIC COMPOSITION

%

72 Indo-Aryan
25 Dravidian
3 Mongoloid and others

Source: Government of India 1986

RELIGIOUS PERSUASION

%

81.3 Hindu
12 Muslim
2.3 Christian
1.9 Sikh
2.5 Others

Source: Government of India, 1997

POPULATION DENSITY

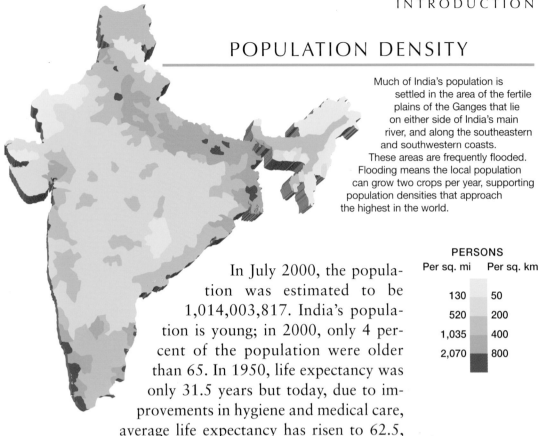

Much of India's population is settled in the area of the fertile plains of the Ganges that lie on either side of India's main river, and along the southeastern and southwestern coasts. These areas are frequently flooded. Flooding means the local population can grow two crops per year, supporting population densities that approach the highest in the world.

PERSONS

Per sq. mi	Per sq. km
130	50
520	200
1,035	400
2,070	800

In July 2000, the population was estimated to be 1,014,003,817. India's population is young; in 2000, only 4 percent of the population were older than 65. In 1950, life expectancy was only 31.5 years but today, due to improvements in hygiene and medical care, average life expectancy has risen to 62.5, and is almost identical for men and women.

Religion: A Part of Life

Religion is woven into every aspect of life in India, although there is no state, or official, religion. The country is the birthplace of two of the world's oldest religions—Hinduism and Buddhism. Today, 80 percent of Indians are Hindu, 12 percent are Muslim, 2.3 percent Christian, about 2 percent Sikh, and 0.8 percent are Buddhist. Jainism, one of the world's smallest religions, is almost exclusive to India (*see* p. 115). Jainism originated in the country at around the same time as Buddhism and comprises 0.5 percent of the population.

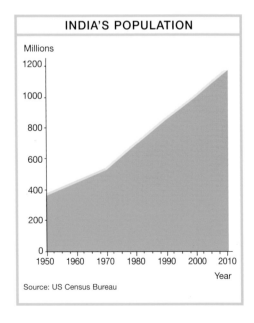

INDIA'S POPULATION

Millions

Source: US Census Bureau

11

Land and Cities

"If there is one place on the face of the earth where all the dreams of living men have found a home from the very earliest days when man began the dream of existence, it is India."

French scholar Romain Rolland

India is a little larger than one-half the size of the United States. It lies within the Indian subcontinent, which is bigger than Europe. From the snow-covered peaks of the Himalaya Mountains, in the north, to India's tropical southern tip, is a distance of some 3,500 miles (5,600 km). The country is divided almost exactly in two by the Tropic of Cancer.

India is the largest country in the Indian subcontinent. Before India gained independence from the British in 1947 (*see* p. 70), the country was even bigger because the present-day countries of Bangladesh and Pakistan then lay within its borders. India is the seventh-largest country in the world after Russia, Canada, China, the United States, Brazil, and Australia. India's total land area is approximately 2,042,870 square miles (3,287,590 sq. km).

India shares land borders with Bangladesh, Bhutan, Myanmar (Burma), China, Nepal, and Pakistan in the north, and is bordered by sea to the west, south, and east. India's mountainous north has traditionally given it a certain amount of protection against invasion, while its coastal areas have since ancient times been important in international trade. Part of the northwestern region is also claimed by Pakistan. India is also in dispute with China over territory along its northeastern border which was taken by China in conflicts in the 1960s.

Women wash clothes on the banks of Lake Bhutanatha in Karnataka State in southwest India as their ancestors have done for centuries.

FACT FILE

● The Himalaya Mountains, which form part of India's northern border, are the highest in the world, although the highest mountain, Everest, lies in Nepal and China.

● The Ganges Plain, in eastern India, is the largest river plain in the world.

● The Asiatic lion is found in only one place in the world—the Gir National Park in the western state of Gujarat.

● A banyan tree in the botanical gardens in Kolkata (Calcutta) has the largest canopy of any tree in the world with a circumference of over 1,300 feet (400 m).

INDIA'S TERRAIN

Mountains
The highest mountain range in the world, the Himalayas stretch into neighboring Pakistan, Nepal, Bhutan, and China. The mountains were created by the Indian peninsula moving northward and thrusting up against the Eurasian Plate— a process which is still happening.

Deccan Plateau
This plateau forms the bulk of the peninsula between the Arabian Sea and the Bay of Bengal. It averages between 1,000 and 2,500 feet (305 and 762 m) above sea level.

Eastern and Western Ghats
These mountain ranges lie along India's southeastern and southwestern coasts. Those in the west are higher and include the Nilgiri Hills, where the highest peak stands at 8,842 feet (2,695 m).

Indo-Gangetic Plain
Located in the foothills of the Himalayas, this vast plain is formed around the Ganges and Brahmaputra rivers. The land slopes very gently toward the river and the lower land with its more recent alluvial soils (rich soils washed down by the river) is more fertile than the older deposits higher up.

A LAND OF CONTRASTS

Almost every variation in geography and climate exists within India. In the frozen Himalaya Mountains are glaciers; in the western states of Gujarat and Rajasthan is the Thar Desert, one of the driest places on earth. To the east in Meghalaya are the world's two wettest cities, Cherrapunji and Mawsynram. The Ganges Plain, in the east, is one of the world's most fertile places. The tapering southern part of India comprises the Deccan Plateau, bordered on both sides by mountains known as the Western and Eastern Ghats.

The Roof of the World

The Himalayas create a massive natural barrier between India and its huge neighbor, China. The mountain range stretches 1,553 miles (2,484 km) from the state of

The Himalayas are named from the Sanskrit words *hima*, meaning "snow" and *laya*, meaning "abode."

Jammu and Kashmir, in the northwest, to the state of Assam, to the southeast. From north to south, the mountains are between 93 and 250 miles (148 and 400 km) wide. The Himalayas actually comprise three parallel ranges of mountains. It is the youngest mountain range in the world, having started to form about 40 million years ago. More than 90 percent of the Himalayan peaks stand over 19,685 feet (6,000 m). India's highest mountain—and the third-highest in the world—

The Himalayas are sacred to Buddhists and cairns (piles of stones) are placed to mark the most sacred places.

Kangchenjunga, is 28,169 feet (8,586 m) high. The highest mountains in the Himalayas are covered in snow year-round. Between the mountain ranges are deep gorges and valleys that are home to many people.

Many of the most important rivers of the subcontinent originate in the snowy Himalayas. The Ganges River, considered holy by the country's Hindu population, starts in the mountains as pure melted snow before flowing southward through India before turning eastward to empty into the Bay of Bengal. The Ganges is joined by many other rivers on its journey south. It is 1,560 miles (2,511 km) long. The seasonal flow of the Ganges, with its melted water flowing down from the Himalayas, make it an important irrigation resource for the surrounding region.

The State of Kashmir

One of the most beautiful states in all of the Himalayas is Kashmir. It is home to the Kashmir goat, which provides the wool for one of the world's costliest materials—cashmere. When the Mughals ruled India (*see* p. 52), they would go to the mountains to escape from the heat in Delhi, where temperatures often reached 104°F (40°C). Their favorite place was Kashmir. Later, the British rulers also escaped the heat of the plains and headed for higher elevations, known as hill stations, where they built summer homes. However, the ruler, or maharaja, of Kashmir forbade the British to build houses on his land. Instead, they built luxurious houseboats, which they moored on the large lake in Srinagar, the state capital. After the British left India, the houseboats became popular with Indian honeymooners and foreign travelers.

After independence in 1947, there was tension between India and Pakistan over which country should own Kashmir. Pakistan, which is a Muslim country, thought it should be part of its territory, and India, which is mainly Hindu, claimed it as its own. Kashmir had Hindu rulers but a predominantly Muslim population. The two countries went to war immediately after India's independence and on three subsequent occasions, in 1965–1966, 1971, and 1999. Kashmiri separatists, who want to make Kashmir an independent nation, joined the conflict. Today the region is still in dispute.

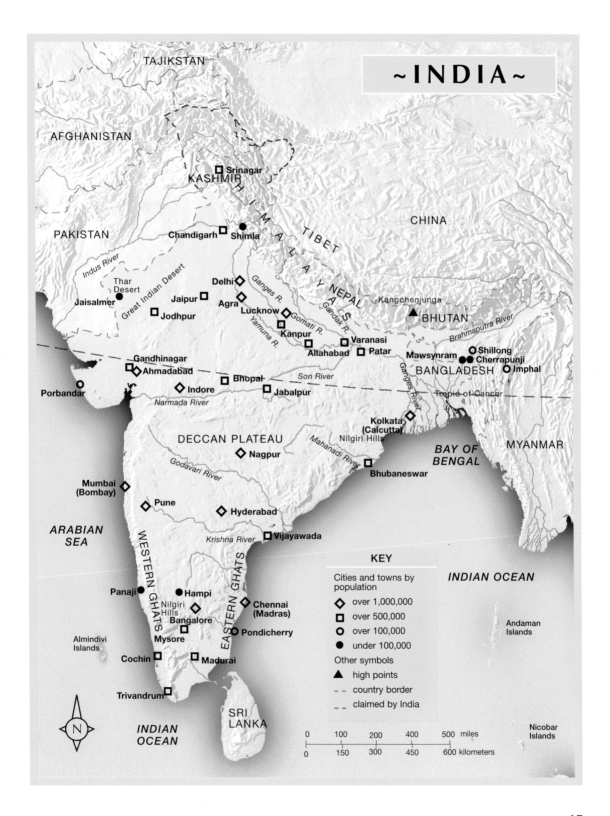

~INDIA~

TAJIKSTAN

AFGHANISTAN

CHINA

PAKISTAN

KASHMIR

HIMALAYAS

TIBET

□ Srinagar

Chandigarh □ ● Shimla

Indus River

Thar Desert

Great Indian Desert

Jaisalmer ●

Jaipur □

Jodhpur ●

Delhi ◇

Ganges R.

Agra ◇

Lucknow □

Yamuna R.

Gomati R.

Gandak R.

NEPAL

Kangchenjunga ▲

BHUTAN

Brahmaputra River

Kanpur □

Varanasi

Allahabad □ Patar □

Mawsynram ○ Shillong

● ● Cherrapunji

Gandhinagar □

Ahmadabad □

BANGLADESH

□ Imphal

Porbandar ○

Indore ●

Bhopal □

Jabalpur □

Son River

Narmada River

Ganges River

Tropic of Cancer

DECCAN PLATEAU

Nagpur ◇

Mahanadi River

Nilgiri Hills

Kolkata (Calcutta) ◇

BAY OF BENGAL

MYANMAR

Godavari River

Bhubaneswar □

Mumbai (Bombay) ◇

Pune ◇

Hyderabad ◇

Krishna River

Vijayawada □

ARABIAN SEA

WESTERN GHATS

EASTERN GHATS

INDIAN OCEAN

Panaji ●

Nilgiri Hills

Bangalore ◇

Hampi ●

Chennai (Madras) ◇

Andaman Islands

Almindivi Islands

Mysore □

Pondicherry ○

Cochin □

Madurai □

Trivandrum □

SRI LANKA

N

INDIAN OCEAN

Nicobar Islands

KEY

Cities and towns by population

◇ over 1,000,000

□ over 500,000

○ over 100,000

● under 100,000

Other symbols

▲ high points

– – country border

– – claimed by India

0	100	200	400	500	miles
0	150	300	450	600	kilometers

The Ganges Plain

The state of Uttar Pradesh in the northeast is India's most populous state. Dominated by the Ganges River and containing four of Hinduism's seven holy towns, it has a population of 139 million.

The area immediately south of the Himalaya range is one of the most fertile areas of land in the world. It extends from Kolkata (formerly Calcutta), in the east, north to the capital, Delhi, toward the Himalayan foothills, and west toward the state of Rajasthan. The area is almost completely flat—Delhi is only 650 feet (200 m) above sea level—and was formed by sediment, washed down from the emerging Himalaya range 40 million years ago. Today the silt and debris are more than 16,400 feet (5,000 m) deep in some areas and holds some of the largest reserves of underground water in the world. Each year, rivers carry and deposit huge quantities of sand and clay, called alluvium, which renews the plain's fertility. The underground water reserves allow the land to be irrigated over a wide area. The plains sustain one of the densest concentrations of population in the world.

The deltas of West Bengal and the southern part of India's neighbor Bangladesh are only 5,000 years old. They were created by huge silt deposits flowing into the Ganges River faster than the sea could remove them. As the silt deposits built up, land was created. The sediment does not reach into western India, with the result that the arid area of India's great desert, the Thar, was formed.

The sand dunes near Sam village in the Thar Desert have been turned into a national park and the area is now a popular destination for camel safaris.

The Ganges River

The Ganges is more than just a river to Hindus—it is their holiest river. Every Hindu wants to make a pilgrimage to the Ganges at some point in his or her life. A fundamental Hindu belief is reincarnation—that is, the idea that when we die, we are endlessly reborn in another body, not always a human one (*see* p. 114). Hindus believe that bathing in the river washes away the sins not only of the present life but of all previous lives. The holiest place to bathe in the Ganges is the northeastern city of Varanasi (above), one of the world's oldest continuously inhabited cities. If Hindus are not able to bathe in the Ganges during their lifetime, they hope to have their ashes scattered in the waters at Varanasi after death. This, they believe, ends the cycle of rebirth.

Varanasi's riverbanks are a spectacular sight. The steps leading down to the river are known as ghats. There are more than a hundred ghats along this stretch of the Ganges. There are ghats for bathing, praying, washing, laundry, and cremation of the dead. A boat trip at dawn, as the sun rises, is the best time to see all these activities.

The Deccan Plateau

South of the Ganges Plain is the arid, high plateau known as the Deccan Plateau, which tapers down to southern India. It is bordered on each side by the Western and Eastern Ghats, ranges of hills running parallel to the coasts. The Western Ghats are higher than the Eastern Ghats and have a wider coastal strip that includes the states of Goa and Kerala. The Ghats taper south and meet toward the tip of India in the Nilgiri Hills.

The Nilgiri Hills in the south are named after the blue haze that seems to hang over the uplands. Nilgiri means "Blue Mountains."

The landscape of the Deccan Plateau is rocky, and the Marathas (*see* p. 55) built impregnable fortresses on the plateau's flat tops. The surface of the Deccan Plateau has been eroded by rivers, such as the Krishna, that flow across the plateau from west to east, emptying into the Bay of Bengal. The rivers produce spectacular gorges with waterfalls that dry up in the dry season and become rushing torrents of water during the rainy monsoon season (*see* p. 24). In Maharashtra state in western India are the Buddhist caves of Ajanta. Their walls are painted with murals that date from 200 B.C. to A.D. 650. Nearby are the later Buddhist, Hindu, and Jain caves of Ellora (*see* p. 96). Thorn forest and scrub cover the inland areas and the eastern parts of the plateau.

In contrast to the Deccan Plateau, the Nilgiri Hills are lush and fertile and are covered with spice forests, coffee bushes, and tea plantations. The southern state of Tamil Nadu is known as the rice bowl of India because there are many green rice fields, called paddy fields. The western coastal states of Kerala and Goa are also green and fertile and are covered in rain forest. Kerala's distinctive landscape is dotted with coconut palms, rubber trees, and canals, or backwaters, that make traveling by boat the best way to get around. Goa, north of Kerala, has rice fields and tropical fruit trees, such as mango and papaya.

Fishing nets like these at Kerala were introduced by the Chinese. It was through Kerala, historically a major trading area, that Chinese ideas and products were taken to the West.

ADMINISTRATIVE DIVISIONS

India is divided into 28 states, covering large areas of the country, and seven smaller union territories, which are either island groups or distinct city areas. Each state has a governor, whose role is mostly ceremonial and a legislative assembly based on the national parliament with a council of ministers led by a chief minister. Below state level, administration is divided into districts, these are then divided into community-level blocks consisting of about 100 villages.

THE STATES OF INDIA

India is divided into 28 states and seven union territories. These are listed below, with the capital of each region marked with a dot on the map on the left. Chandigarh is capital of Haryana, Punjab, and the union territory of Chandigarh.

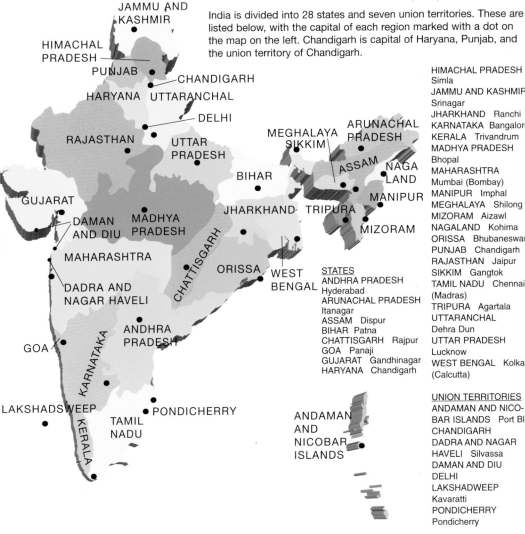

HIMACHAL PRADESH
Simla
JAMMU AND KASHMIR
Srinagar
JHARKHAND Ranchi
KARNATAKA Bangalore
KERALA Trivandrum
MADHYA PRADESH
Bhopal
MAHARASHTRA
Mumbai (Bombay)
MANIPUR Imphal
MEGHALAYA Shilong
MIZORAM Aizawl
NAGALAND Kohima
ORISSA Bhubaneswar
PUNJAB Chandigarh
RAJASTHAN Jaipur
SIKKIM Gangtok
TAMIL NADU Chennai
(Madras)
TRIPURA Agartala
UTTARANCHAL
Dehra Dun
UTTAR PRADESH
Lucknow
WEST BENGAL Kolkata
(Calcutta)

STATES
ANDHRA PRADESH
Hyderabad
ARUNACHAL PRADESH
Itanagar
ASSAM Dispur
BIHAR Patna
CHATTISGARH Rajpur
GOA Panaji
GUJARAT Gandhinagar
HARYANA Chandigarh

UNION TERRITORIES
ANDAMAN AND NICO-
BAR ISLANDS Port Blair
CHANDIGARH
DADRA AND NAGAR
HAVELI Silvassa
DAMAN AND DIU
DELHI
LAKSHADWEEP
Kavaratti
PONDICHERRY
Pondicherry

INDIA'S CLIMATE

India is such a huge country that it contains many different types of climate and geographical features. It is quite possible for it to be snowing in the Himalayas while, in the south, the sun beats down and temperatures can rise to more than 104°F (40°C). In the desert state of Rajasthan during the 1980s, no rain fell for several years, leading to drought and water rationing for the local people. In contrast, the city of Mawsynram, in Meghalaya state in northeast India, is the wettest place on earth.

India lies in the northern hemisphere and so its seasons—spring, summer, fall, and winter—occur at the same time as they do in North America. The seasons change according to the arrival and departure of the monsoon (*see* box p. 24). Spring falls between February and April; then temperatures rise until the heat and humidity become so stifling during the Indian summer that the monsoon rains provide a welcome relief. Once the rains finish during September and October, the temperature drops and conditions are once again more comfortable. In the capital city, Delhi, it is cool enough for people to wear sweaters in December and January, but the south stays constantly hot throughout the year.

Because the Indian peninsula is still moving northward, thrusting under the Eurasian Plate, the area of the Himalayas and other ranges to the east are prone to earthquakes, and landslides are common.

Kolkota experiences constant temperatures throughout the year and extremes of rainfall, while in Delhi temperatures drop significantly in winter.

RAINFALL AND TEMPERATURE

The Monsoon

The word monsoon is Arabic for "season." It describes the rains that arrive in India each year between June and October. The monsoon is caused by the wind changing direction. The northeasterly winds that normally sweep across India bringing dry air from Central Asia are replaced by wet and warm southwesterly winds. The Indian monsoon is unique because of its regularity and the amount of moisture that passes over the country. During the monsoon, it usually rains every day. By the end of September, dry, brown-baked land has turned green and lush, although most of the monsoon rains run straight into the sea. The monsoon clouds have an average depth of 19,685 feet (6,000 m) compared to only 6,560 feet (2,000 m) during the summer rains in Japan. The rains decrease the farther north the monsoon travels, particularly toward the northwest, which remains comparatively dry. The southern state of Tamil Nadu does not receive its rains during the summer monsoon. Instead, the retreating monsoon, now blowing from the northeast, brings heavy rains between the months of October and December.

There are many myths about the Indian monsoon. One is that it always arrives on June 1 in Thiruvananthapuram, the largest southernmost city. In fact the monsoon can arrive at any date. When the monsoon fails to arrive, serious consequences follow, such as the drought that hit Rajasthan in the 1980s.

ANIMALS AND PLANTS

India is home to unique species of plants and animals that are some of the most spectacular in the world. There are more than 500 species of mammals in India, more than 2,000 species of birds, and 30,000 species of insects. Animals are part of Indian daily life. Two of the most popular gods in the Hindu religion are the monkey god, Hanuman, and the elephant god, Ganesh.

In India's cities, cows, considered sacred by the Hindus, wander freely in the streets amid the buses and taxis. In the countryside, the black-faced langur monkey with its long tail and the rhesus macaque monkey with its orange-red behind play in trees next to villages. Animals are never far away in India, largely because people have moved into the animals' habitat and the limited space has forced humans and animals to live side by side.

The destruction of the natural habitat has started to have disastrous consequences for India's animals. The Indian elephant, the tiger, and the Asiatic lion are still found in India today, but poaching and the growing human population threaten the survival of many species. Some animals, such as the cheetah, are already extinct in India.

Holy Cows

Cows have been worshiped in India since ancient times. The cow represents nurturing and fertility. It is linked to the mother goddess and is a symbol of Mother India itself. The sacred cow is the deity Khamdenu and cow dung and urine are used in India to purify the home (the urine wards off insects). Each part of the cow's body is seen as significant. The horns symbolize the gods, the face the sun and moon, the shoulders Agni (the god of fire), and the legs the Himalayas.

National Parks and Project Tiger

India recognized the threat to its wildlife in the 1970s and began creating national parks to preserve the natural world. Today, there are almost 70 national parks and 330 sanctuaries spread across India.

Tigers once roamed across the whole of India. At the start of the 20th century, the estimated tiger population stood at 40,000. When the British ruled India

The tiger is India's national animal and the country is unique in having both lions and tigers. Conservationists argue that the amount India spends on wildlife (equivalent to 0.2% of its GDP) should be increased because the country is so important ecologically.

(*see* p. 58), tiger hunts were a popular sport for the British and wealthy Indians. One hundred tigers a day would be killed. Today, it is estimated that there are only 7,000 tigers left in the world, of which half are in India. Project Tiger was started by the Indian government and the World Wildlife Fund to encourage the tiger to breed by giving it protected areas of wilderness. In 1973, 9,650 square miles (25,000 sq. km) was set aside for Project Tiger. There were early successes and the number of tigers increased from a low of 1,800 in the 1970s to 3,500 in the 1990s. However, the tiger is again under threat from ruthless poachers who kill the animal to sell its skin and body parts to the Chinese medicine market.

The national parks are home to many other species of animals in addition to the tiger. The Asiatic lion, which is found only in the Gir National

NATIONAL PARKS

DACHIGAM

CORBETT

DUDHWA   KARIZANGA

NAMDAPHA

SARISKA   KEOLADEO

KEIBUL
LAM JAO

RANTHAMBHOR

GIR

SUNDARABANS

KANHA

SIMLIPAL

BANDIPUR

PERIYAR

India has many national parks and sanctuaries, all administered at state level. In addition to the larger nature reserves, there are also a number of reserves set up to provide a safe environment for the country's threatened lion and tiger populations. The national parks are now seen by regional governments as a way of attracting tourists, and special efforts are being made to provide accommodations and adequate transportation, although facilities vary tremendously between regions. All of the national parks are closed during the monsoon season.

Park in Gujarat state, differs from its African relative in having no shaggy mane. A visitor to a national park might see leopards, panthers, elephants (*see* box p. 28), Indian one-horned rhinoceroses, different species of deer—such as the sambar, swamp deer, and spotted deer—antelopes, black bulls, gazelles, water buffalos, bison, and, in the Himalayas, yaks.

In the countryside, jackals and hyenas scavenge, and birds such as vultures and crows sit in the branches of trees. The Gangetic dolphin swims in the Ganges River, and the sloth bear, with its long snout, lives in forests. The sloth bear is often caught and used by street entertainers to earn money from its "dancing."

India has a huge variety of birdlife that varies according to the climate. Doves, crows, and vultures are a common sight in Indian cities. In the swamps of India, cormorants, cranes, and storks are to be found. The most common and perhaps prettiest waterbird is the kingfisher, which has an orange breast and bright blue upper body. Birds such as

The Indian Elephant

The Indian elephant is smaller than its African relative, and is the second-largest land mammal after the African elephant. Its ears are smaller and the female is tuskless. Sometimes even the male Indian elephant does not have tusks. The Indian elephant is revered in the Hindu religion and is valued for its hard work in daily life. It is not unusual to see an elephant at work in rural areas, carrying goods with its trunk or dragging logs. The elephant has been used by people for about 5,000 years, and each elephant has a boy, called a *mahout*, who looks after the animal. Looking after an elephant can be hard work—a working elephant needs to be fed for about 18 hours a day by hand. It eats between 220 and 660 pounds (100 and 300 kg) of vegetation every day. Wild elephants can be dangerous if they come into contact with humans. They often destroy buildings and crops.

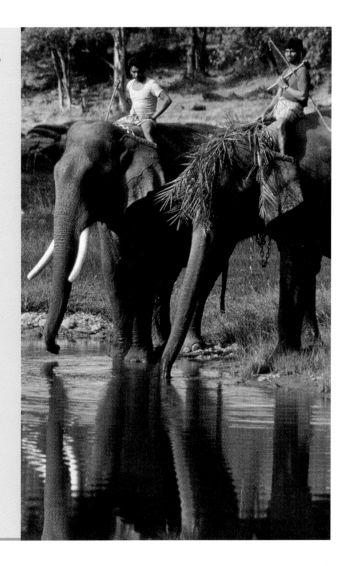

the egret, myna, and parakeet live in the grasslands, while at higher altitudes are magpies, wagtails, and pheasants.

India is also home to many types of reptiles, including large snakes such as the Indian rock python and the king cobra. In houses all over India, the gecko, a small lizard, is a frequent visitor and comes out at night to catch insects. Crocodiles live in some of the country's rivers, the most common of these fearsome reptiles are the mugger, or marsh, crocodiles, and the gharial, which live in freshwater. The gharial is between 19 and 26 feet (6 and 8 m) long, twice the size of the mugger.

India has over 2,000 species of fish. Sharks are found in the country's coastal waters and even venture inland along some of the major rivers.

Among India's most distinctive features are its colorful flowers and trees. Flamboyant bougainvillaea trees are seen all over the country with their bright orange, pink, and purple leaves. The frangipani bush's white flowers have a sweet scent and are also very common, as is the colorful hibiscus plant with its trumpet-shaped flowers that vary from scarlet to yellow. Imported from Brazil, the jacaranda tree with its blue-purple flowers lines town and country roads, as does the yellow-and-red-flowered tamarind tree. Coconut palm trees and fruit trees grow all over the south and coastal parts of India.

In the Himalayas, alpine flowers and trees such as pine, spruce, and fir are commonly found. The most famous tree in India is the banyan—the Indian fig tree. It is planted by temples, in villages, and alongside roads. Another typical Indian tree—the bodhi—owes its fame to the Buddha (*see* p. 114), who is said to have reached enlightenment (religious wisdom) beneath its branches.

The banyan tree spreads by aerial roots that hang down from its branches. These reach down to the ground to form new trunks, so that one tree may eventually appear like a dense thicket of trunks.

INDIA'S CITIES

Although India is predominantly a rural country—75 percent of the population live in the countryside—almost 250 million people live in India's cities. The major cities all continue to grow rapidly as people from the countryside flock to them daily in search of work. Despite being the capital city, Delhi does not have the largest population—both Mumbai (Bombay) and Kolkata (Calcutta) are larger. People living on the streets is a common sight in every major city, and shanty towns—shacks built of discarded materials—house thousands in every city. Some smaller cities, such as the southern city of Bangalore, grew very rapidly at the end of the 20th century. The immigrants to Bangalore are mostly highly educated university graduates who work in the computer technology field.

Mumbai

The city of Mumbai used to be called Bombay. It lies on India's west coast and is India's largest city with a population of over 15 million. It is also the country's

A view of the city of Mumbai with the docks in the background.

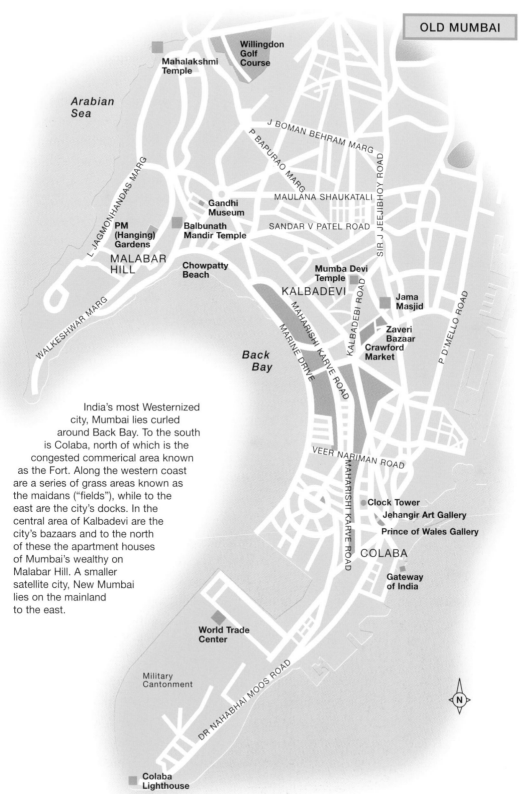

Arabian
Sea

Mahalakshmi
Temple

Willingdon
Golf
Course

J BOMAN BEHRAM MARG

P BAPURAO MARG

L JAGMONHANDAS MARG

MAULANA SHAUKATALI

SIR J JEEJIBHOY ROAD

Gandhi
Museum

PM
(Hanging)
Gardens

Balbunath
Mandir Temple

SANDAR V PATEL ROAD

MALABAR
HILL

Chowpatty
Beach

Mumba Devi
Temple

KALBADEVI

KALBADEBI ROAD

Jama
Masjid

WALKESHWAR MARG

MAHARISHI KARVE ROAD

MARINE DRIVE

Zaveri
Bazaar
Crawford
Market

P D'MELLO ROAD

Back
Bay

India's most Westernized
city, Mumbai lies curled
around Back Bay. To the south
is Colaba, north of which is the
congested commerical area known
as the Fort. Along the western coast
are a series of grass areas known as
the maidans ("fields"), while to the
east are the city's docks. In the
central area of Kalbadevi are the
city's bazaars and to the north
of these the apartment houses
of Mumbai's wealthy on
Malabar Hill. A smaller
satellite city, New Mumbai
lies on the mainland
to the east.

VEER NARIMAN ROAD

MAHARISHI KARVE ROAD

Clock Tower
Jehangir Art Gallery
Prince of Wales Gallery

COLABA

Gateway
of India

World Trade
Center

Military
Cantonment

DR NAHABHAI MOOS ROAD

N

Colaba
Lighthouse

Dhaba Wallahs

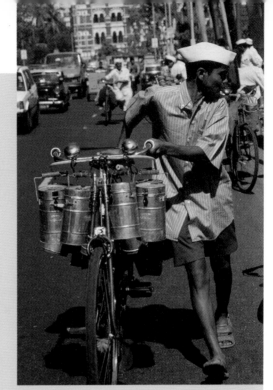

One of Mumbai's unique features is the dhaba wallahs. Each day at around midday, the dhaba wallahs gather at the suburban rail stations. They are waiting for the arrival of thousands of tiffin, or lunchboxes, which they then deliver to individual office workers. The system works like this—in the suburbs a worker's wife prepares his daily lunch of rice, vegetables, and dhal (lentil curry) and packs it into the heat-retaining metal tiffin boxes. The boxes are then transported by train to Mumbai where the dhaba wallahs collect them and distribute them. It is unusual for a tiffin box to get lost or be late due to a simple color-coded system that tells the illiterate dhaba wallahs where to distribute and then collect the lunch boxes, which are later transported back to the suburbs.

financial and commercial center and home to one of India's biggest industries, the movies. This industry is known as "Bollywood." The film industry attracts many aspiring actors to the city, who come in the hope of superstardom.

Like New York City's Manhattan, Mumbai is an island, attached to the mainland by numerous bridges. Mumbai was created from seven islands made into one through land reclamation. The island is no wider than 3 miles (5 km) and 14 miles (22 km) long at any one point. It is bordered on three sides by the Arabian Sea. Into this small area are squeezed many of the city's inhabitants, its industries, docks, warehouses, and major businesses. The city is expanding rapidly and part of the mainland forms the greater Mumbai suburbs. Mumbai has the largest shantytown in Asia, called Dharvi, which is home to approximately one million people. Known as "tin towns" because of the flimsy shacks' corrugated tin roofs, the shanty towns have inadequate sewerage, limited running water, and no paved sidewalks. They are home to illiterate manual workers from the countryside.

Mumbai has some of the highest rent prices anywhere in the world, and for many, even a shanty home is unaffordable. For years whole families lived on central Mumbai's streets—cooking, sleeping, and eating in the open—but recent efforts to clean up the city have resulted in these families being moved out of the city center.

In a city where money is so important, one of its most enjoyable places is free. As dusk falls, families gather on Chowpatty Beach to walk, sit, or enjoy a snack from one of the many *bhelpuri* vendors operating on the beach. *Bhelpuri* is made of noodles, puffed rice, and wheat crackers mixed with diced boiled potatoes (*see* p. 110). Fortune-tellers, masseurs, monkey trainers, hand-operated Ferris wheels, and food-sellers are all to be found on the beach.

Mumbai life moves at a fast pace. The streets are choked with cars, black-and-yellow taxis, red buses with two levels, called double-deckers, scooters, auto-rickshaws, and even the odd cow. Office workers pour in and out of the city's railroad stations. Between two and three million workers travel to the city each day. Many commute for up to two hours a day on overcrowded trains because they cannot afford the high rents of the city center.

Mumbai's Chowpatty Beach is a long, semi-circular shaped beach on the Arabian Sea. At night the bay is all lit up. From the top of nearby Malabar Hill it looks like a necklace of lights—hence its nickname, the "queen's necklace."

Delhi

India's governmental and administrative capital is Delhi. The difference between Mumbai and Delhi is equivalent to that between New York and Washington, D.C. That is, although Delhi is the capital, it is not the largest city in India and neither is it the financial and commercial center. With nine million inhabitants, Delhi is India's third-largest city.

What is now modern Delhi has been the site of more than a dozen cities from around the ninth century B.C. Present-day Delhi consists of two parts: Old Delhi, which was the capital under the Mughals (*see* p. 52) between the 17th and 19th centuries, and New Delhi, which was created by the British when they decided to move the capital from Kolkata (Calcutta) in 1911. New Delhi is distinguished from other Indian cities by its broad avenues and green spaces, although the sense of space is being diminished as the population expands rapidly. Old Delhi, in contrast, is more like other Indian cities with its narrow streets and bustling activity.

The Indian flag flies above the battlements of Delhi's Red Fort. The fort was built over ten years, from 1638 to 1648, the period of the greatest Mughal power in the region.

Old Delhi lies to the north of the city, and is dominated by the Red Fort, the massive center of Mughal government completed in 1648, and by the Jami Masjid, India's largest mosque. Off Chandni Chowk run Delhi's bazaars, selling everything from spices to silver and from car parts to chickens. South of the bazaars lies New Delhi. Since 1931 the center of India's national government, New Delhi's tree-lined avenues contrast sharply with the bustle to the north. Southern Delhi, a rapidly expanding suburban area, contains the remains of several of Delhi's ancient cities.

DELHI

Yamuna River

Fatepuri Mosque
National Museum
CHANDNI CHOWK
Red Fort
QUTB ROAD
Jami Masjid (Mosque)
New Delhi Railway Station
Delhi Gate
MANDIR MARG
Ashoka Pillar
CONNAUGHT PLACE
VIRAS MARG
SANSAD MARG
Yamuna River
NEW DELHI
RAJPATH NAME
Parliament
Rashtrapati Bhavan
RAJ PATH
India Gate
MATHURA ROAD
Secretariat
National Museum
National Gallery of Modern Art
Nehru Museum
Indira Gandhi Memorial
Lodi Gardens
LODI ROAD
Humayun's Tomb
LALA LAJPAT RAI PATH
RING ROAD
MATHURA ROAD
AFRICA AVENUE
Deer Park
Moti Baugh Mosque
Bahai Temple
Kalkaji Temple
SRI AUROBINDO MARG
Siri
PANCHSHEEL MARG
Qutab Minar Complex
MEHRAULI BADARPUR ROAD
Tughluqabad

N

The symbol of the swastika, more famous in Europe and the United States for its use by the German Nazis, was originally an ancient Aryan symbol of perfection. Many Hindu temples include the symbol in their design.

Delhi has always played an important part in India's history. Its northerly position gave it strategic importance because India's numerous invaders entered the country from the north. An old saying is that whoever founds a new city at Delhi will eventually lose control of it, and the saying has been proven right each time. Today, Delhi is one of India's fastest-growing cities as rural workers flock to it in search of work.

Old Delhi was laid out by Emperor Shah Jahan in about 1640 as a walled city. Shah Jahan was a Mughal ruler who reigned from 1627 to 1658. Naturally enough, Old Delhi contains many of the oldest streets, buildings, and monuments in Delhi. The Lal Qila, or Red Fort, is a massive, red sandstone fort containing palaces and halls. It was the seat of the Mughal emperors (*see* p. 52) and once contained the fabulous solid gold, jewel-encrusted Peacock Throne. Facing the fort is

Delhi's Seven Cities

The importance of Delhi in northern India is borne out by the several ancient cities founded in and around the present capital. The earliest of these was built to the southwest of modern Delhi in A.D. 736 and named Lal Kot by its Tomara Rajput founders. It was captured by a rival clan in 1180 and given its present name of Qila Rai Pithora. In 1290, the Turkish Khaljis came to power, establishing the second city of Siri to the east in 1303, which rapidly became a thriving commercial center. Another fortress was built to the east of the original city a few years later, but was swiftly abandoned because of a lack of water. In 1327 a fourth city, Jahanpanah was built between Lal Kot and Siri and a fifth, Firozabad was built in 1354. It was not until the 16th century that the sixth city, the fort of Din-Panah (now known as Purana Qila) was built by the Afghan king Sher Shah, who had driven out the ruling sultan Humayun; the latter reclaimed the city in 1555. The seventh city, the magnificent new walled capital of Shajahanabad was built by Shah Jahan in the 17th century. Parts of this complex, encompassing the Red Fort and the Jama Masjid, or Friday Mosque, is now known as Old Delhi. Only with the building of the planned city of New Delhi were Delhi's earlier cities finally joined into one vast urban center.

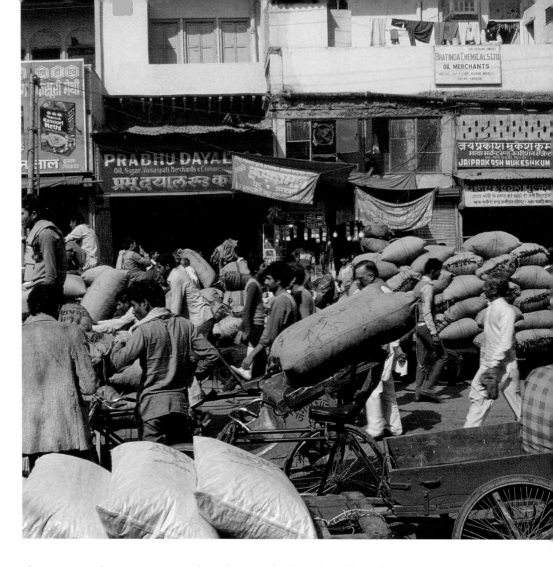

the ancient bazaar, or marketplace, of Chandni Chowk with its narrow maze of crowded alleys running off the main street. Chandni Chowk bustles with shops selling gold, spices, clothes, and many other goods. The best way to explore Chandni Chowk is by rickshaw, which can be hired very cheaply.

Less than a mile (1.6 km) from the Red Fort is the Jama Masjid, or Friday Mosque, which was the last great architectural work of Shah Jahan. A mosque is a place of worship for Muslims. This is the largest example in India and as many as 20,000 Muslims can pray there at one time. Together with the Red Fort, it dominates the skyline of Old Delhi.

Delhi's bustling Chandni Chowk was once a tree-lined canal. Today it is Old Delhi's main thoroughfare.

Trolleys, cars, taxis, and trucks choke the streets in central Kolkata.

Kolkata

Kolkata, formerly known as Calcutta, is India's second-largest city with a population of 14 million. Kolkata lies on the east coast in the state of Bengal. Compared to India's other major cities, Kolkata is relatively young. It was created 300 years ago by British traders so that their company, the East India Company, could have a port to export its goods. Once the British took political control of India, Kolkata became the capital. With its cathedral, buildings dedicated to the British queen Victoria—who was Empress of India from 1876 to 1901—and colonial architecture, Kolkata resembles an English city more than

The Black Hole of Calcutta

In 1756 the new ruler of Bengal, the young nawab, or prince, Siraj-ud-daula, was eager to seize British-owned gold. He easily captured Calcutta from the British, and all but 146 of the British residents fled. Those who remained were captured and locked overnight in an underground cell with only one tiny window. The outside temperature was over 104°F (40°C). Next morning when the warders unlocked the door, they found 123 men and women had suffocated to death. The British called the incident the "black hole of Calcutta."

an Indian one. It is the only Indian city to have a subway, which opened in 1984.

The center of Kolkata is clustered around the Maidan, one of the largest city parks in the world. Planned at the same time as the military base of Fort William in the 18th century, Maidan contrasts sharply with the overcrowded streets that border it, particularly to the north. On the west bank of the Hooghly River lies the industrial area of Howrah, while the south of the city is largely residential.

Kolkata suffers from a bad image. Many outsiders consider the city of Kolkata to be poor, squalid, and dirty. The charity worker Mother Teresa, who founded her Sisters of Mercy mission to help the poorest people of Kolkata, did so because she saw the most poverty and deprivation in and around the city. While Kolkata's problems are huge, the city is also dynamic and vibrant and is home to many of India's artists and intellectuals. The city has a thriving Bengali theater scene, large Indian classical music festivals, and many art galleries.

KOLKATA

Digambar Jain Temple
BELGACHIA ROAD
N. GHAT STREET
Sitalnath Jain Temple
HOWRAH BRIDGE
Rabindra Bharati
Marble Palace
KESHAR CHANDRA SEN STREET
Hooghly River
STRAND ROAD
Nakhoda Mosque
COLLEGE STREET
Government House
LENIN SARANI
Fort William
CHOWRINGHEE
New Market
Indian Museum
A J C BOSE ROAD
The Maidan
KINDERPORE ROAD
St. Paul's Cathedral
A J C BOSE ROAD
ASHUTOSH CHOWDHURYROAD
National Library
ASHUTOSH MUKHERJEE ROAD
SARAT BOSE ROAD
Kalighat Temple
Rabrindra Sarobar (The Lakes)
N

Chennai

Chennai, formerly known as Madras, is India's fourth-largest city. With a population of nearly six million, Chennai is the largest city in south India. Located on India's east coast in the state of Tamil Nadu, it differs from the other major cities in its slower pace of life compared to its northerly counterparts. It was founded by the British East India Company in 1639 on a narrow 3-mile (5-km) strip of land between the Kuvam (Cooum) and Adyar rivers. Chennai rose to importance as a trading post for the British in the 17th century. Repeatedly attacked by the French during the 18th century, the city was gradually fortified by the British. Its mixture of colonial British buildings and a strong Tamil identity give it a unique quality. The town was renamed Chennai in 1997 to reassert its precolonial identity. The city is a center for Dravidian nationalism, a movement which represents the concerns of the native people of southern India and defends them against the cultural influence of the north and the remnants of India's colonial past.

The bulbous white domes and sandstone towers of the High Court Building at Chennai show strong Islamic influences, despite being built during the colonial period.

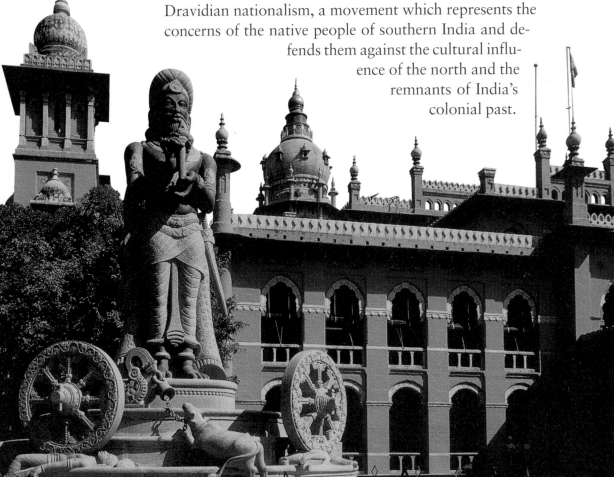

Chennai is divided into three main areas. The northern district consists of the original British settlement, based around George Town, a center for banks, offices, and shipping companies. In the center of the city is the main commercial and residential area, bisected by the main thoroughfare, Anna Salai, and bordered to the east by the 3-mile (5-km) marina. To the south lies Mylapore, a major settlement since ancient times and the site of the 19th-century San Thome Cathedral, built over the tomb of St. Thomas, and the Kapalishvara Temple, dedicated to Shiva and built during the 16th century. During the 1990s, Chennai boomed as India opened up to foreign investment. The disadvantage of this is that the previously tranquil city has rapidly become overcrowded with people who have moved from the countryside to the city to seek work.

CHENNAI

WALTAX ROAD

MINT STREET

George Town

Vepery

High Court

POONAMALLEE HIGH ROAD

Cooum (Kuvam) River

Fort St. George

Egmore

SWAMI SIVANANDA SALAI

WALLAJAH ROAD

KAMARAJAR SALAI

ANNA SALAI

BHARATHI SALAI

Buckingham Canal

PETER'S ROAD

Bay of Bengal

LLOYD'S ROAD

DR RADHAKRISHNAN SALAI

Alwarpet

TTK ROAD

LUZ CHURCH ROAD

Kapalishvara Temple ■

San Thome Cathedral ■

ST. MARY'S ROAD

Nandaman

R K MUTT ROAD

Mylapore

Adyar River

GREENWAY'S ROAD

N

Past and Present

"India is the cradle of the human race, the birthplace of human speech, the mother of history, the grandmother of legend, and the great-grandmother of tradition."

U.S. writer Mark Twain

India has one of the world's oldest civilizations. Historians have found evidence of early human civilization in north India dating back to 2,500 B.C.

Among India's first invaders were the Aryans, who pushed India's original inhabitants, the Dravidians southward. Early Hinduism developed under the Aryans. Later the Mauryans, who were native to India, ruled over an empire that extended over a large part of the Indian subcontinent. About 500 B.C., the religion of Buddhism was born in India. The Gupta empire emerged in the fourth century A.D., and brought with it many new developments in the arts and sciences. Different groups of Muslim invaders arrived in India after the eighth century, the most notable of which were the Mughals, who arrived in India in the 16th century. The Mughal empire saw a flowering of the arts and literature in India, and construction of some of India's most impressive buildings.

The Portuguese were the first Europeans to colonize parts of India, followed by the French, Dutch, Danish, and British. In the 19th century, the British set about making India part of their empire, and by the middle of the century, the British government took overall control of India. For the next 90 years or so, India was part of the British empire and did not gain its independence until 1947. Modern India is a rich mixture of traditional cultures with elements of its different foreign occupiers.

European traders are shown fighting over the spoils of Indian trade. India was the richest country on earth until the arrival of the British in the 17th century.

FACT FILE

● India's civilization stretches back more than 4,500 years.

● The period of the Guptas (A.D. 320–550) to the reign of Harsha Vardhana (A.D. 606–657), during which northern Indian was unified, is known as the Classical Age of Indian history.

● The era of the Gupta empire (*see* p. 49) produced six systems of philosophy—Nyaya, Waissheshika, Sankhya, Yoga, Mimamsa, and Vedanta. Vedanta is still the basis of Indian philosophy.

● Kerala was the first state in the world to elect a communist government democratically (in 1957).

EARLY CIVILIZATIONS

In the 1920s, archaeologists discovered evidence of a developed civilization in India that flourished about 2500 B.C. Archaeological excavations proved that the civilization extended across northwestern and western India (the states of Gujarat and Rajasthan) and the Indus River valley (in present-day Pakistan). Known as the Harappa civilization, its great cities were Harappa and Mohenjodaro, both in present-day Pakistan. Archaeologists uncovered evidence of streets planned on a grid system, a sewage system, zoned housing for different social groups, and public buildings. The people of the Harappa culture developed their own written script, based on pictures, although historians still have to decipher all of the script. The people also worked with metals such as copper, bronze, lead, and tin and made their own bricks in kilns.

The present-day religion of Hinduism has its origins in the religious beliefs of the Harappans. They worshiped male and female gods that are prehistoric versions of Kali, the goddess of destruction, and Siva, the god of both creation and destruction. The Harappa society was ruled by priests rather than kings. This was later reflected in the Hindu caste system (*see* p. 114), where priests were the most respected members of society.

The Harappa civilization lasted for about 1,000 years. Historians do not know precisely why it declined, although it is possible that repeated flooding of the towns

The Indus Civilization

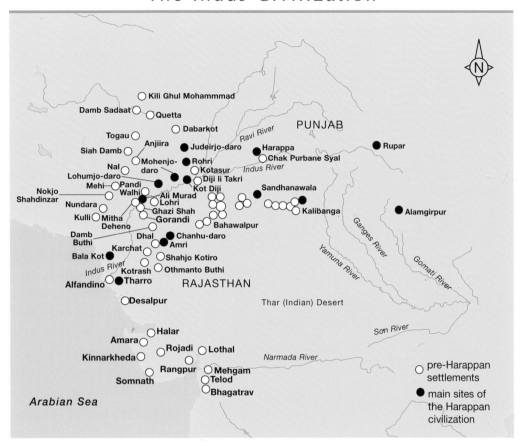

located on the banks of the Indus River and the spread of desert land and droughts contributed to its collapse. By the time the Aryans arrived from the present-day Middle East in 1500 B.C., Harappan culture had all but died out.

The Harappan civilization developed in a relatively small area around the Indus River and was protected from attacks by desert and high mountains.

The Aryan Civilization

The Aryan people invaded India from Central Asia and moved south between 1500 and 200 B.C. Although the Ayrans pushed the Dravidians, India's original inhabitants, south, the Aryans never controlled south India, which developed separately from north India. Many of the elements of modern-day India have their roots in Aryan civilization. For example, the Sanskrit language, the caste system, a village-based agricultural society, and

The Vedic Scriptures

The Vedic Scriptures form the basis of the Hindu religion. They were written between 1500 and 1200 B.C. *Veda* means divine knowledge. The four *Vedas*—*Rigveda, Yajurveda, Samaveda,* and *Atharvaveda*— are a collection of hymns and religious texts. They were composed as hymns, or religious homages, to the magnificent Himalaya Mountains, the lush river valleys, the green forests of ancient India, and the divine power that created such beauty. Although the Aryans worshiped many gods, the *Vedas* reveal that the Aryans believed all the gods to be manifestations, or appearances, of one divine power. This idea underlies contemporary Hindu belief (*see* p. 113).

the origins of the Hindu religion all date from this period. The Aryans were the first invaders to build their capital at Delhi.

The Aryans worked as farmers and raised cattle. The people whose land they had invaded were made to work in the fields, plowing the land with oxen and cultivating crops such as barley, cucumber, and sugarcane. The Aryans became wealthy through their farming and through the use of slave labor. With plenty of free time, they turned their attentions to pursuing philosophical questions. The search for answers about the human position in the universe was linked to the Ayrans' religious worship of gods of nature. That is, they believed that humans were part of nature and that all nature was divine. They developed a sophisticated spoken language, Sanskrit, but were slow to develop writing. Instead, they passed on information orally.

The Aryans were organized into tribes each with an hereditary chief. The tribes were then divided along caste lines. Caste was the name given to the grouping of Hindu society into four main divisions. Originally, the division was based on color, with the fair-skinned Aryans favored over the dark-skinned Dravidian slaves. This was called the *varna* (color) division. The Aryans then were subdivided into the following groups, or castes, according to their occupation: the Brahmins (priests), *Kshatriyas* (warriors), *Vaishyas* (farmers), and *Shudras* (menial workers). At first the divisions were flexible and it was possible for people to move from one group to another. Later, a person's caste position was determined at birth and changing from one caste to another became difficult. The caste system continues to exist today (*see* p. 114).

While the Aryans continued to hold power in the north, invaders arrived in other parts of India, including Greece's Alexander the Great (356–323 B.C.). He reached western India in 326 B.C. but his troops refused to march farther than the Beas River, the most easterly point in the Persian empire that Alexander had conquered. He turned back without increasing his empire by conquering India.

The Mauryan Empire

Two centuries before Alexander reached India, an Indian empire had started to develop in the north. The Mauryan empire expanded from its capital in present-day Patna, in Bihar state. India's size, and the fact that the Aryans controlled only part of it, meant it was inevitable that other groups would seize power and expand wherever possible.

The Mauryan empire, named after the ruler Chandragupta Maurya, became the first Indian empire and marked the first unification of the north of the country.

The Mauryans extended their territory into lands in the west left vacant by Alexander's departure. The Mauryan empire controlled northern India from its capital from 321 B.C. until 184 B.C.

The Mauryans were the first native Indians to unify much of India. Those who held power formed an extensive bureaucracy that collected taxes efficiently from the agriculture-based society. The Mauryan rulers used slaves, laborers, and

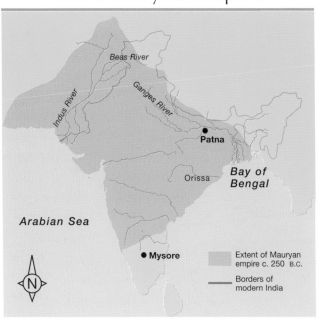

The Mauryan Empire

prisoners to work on their huge farms, while private landowners used paid laborers to till their land—another source of revenue was the gambling houses. The empire reached its peak under the leadership of the emperor Asoka (*see* box below), who was a successful and inspirational leader of his people.

Emperor Asoka

When Asoka (?–232 B.C.) inherited his empire in 272 B.C., it covered the entire Indian subcontinent with the exception of present-day Orissa. The empire stretched from today's Afghanistan to Assam, in the east, and from the Himalayas, in the north, to Mysore, in the south. Shocked by the dead bodies that littered the battlefield after he conquered Orissa, which he had quickly captured, Asoka turned his back on warfare. He became a pacifist (a person who is against warfare) and converted to the relatively new religion of Buddhism.

Buddhism emerged in India about 500 B.C. (*see* p. 114). This new religion rejected the *Vedas* and the caste system of Hinduism. Buddhism teaches that the path to salvation—the goal of every Buddhist—comes by reaching "enlightenment." Enlightenment is a state anybody can reach once they decide no longer to desire worldly things, such as wealth, and to learn moderation in all things. Unlike Hinduism, Buddhism teaches that a person's destiny, or fate, is not predetermined but can be directed by the person.

Asoka made Buddhism the official religion of his empire. In a series of edicts, or public notices, he urged his subjects to follow the code of *dharma*—morality, piety, virtue, and social order. The edicts were inscribed on columns across the empire, some of which survive today. The lion pillar of Asoka is the official emblem of the Republic of India and is found on every rupee note and coin. Following Asoka's death in 232 B.C., the Mauryan empire started to fall apart and by 184 B.C. had collapsed completely.

The South

Events in north India often had little bearing on the south. While Buddhism and, to a lesser extent, the religion of Jainism (*see* p. 115) overtook Hinduism in the north, the south continued to be a Hindu stronghold. The area had developed trading links with the Egyptian, Roman, and Greek empires. It also traded with Southeast Asia and China. Reports of the battles of the warring kings of the Chera, Chola, and ancient Pandya kingdoms in the south formed the basis of a distinctive south Indian literature. Known as Sangam literature, it consisted of poems composed by groups of traveling poets, or minstrels. One assembly of these traveling musicians saw more than 2,000 poems being composed collectively at one time.

The subjugation of the Shakas in Gujarat in western India secured the trade of the western coast and made Gupta India the center of a vast trading network, stretching from China to Europe.

The Gupta Empire

Following the collapse of the Mauryan empire, a period of confusion followed as rival kingdoms rose and fell. The Gupta empire emerged in the fourth century A.D. and brought with it a period of stability and a flourishing of the arts and sciences. Over the next two centuries, the boundaries of the empire changed under different rulers but the period was mostly peaceful. The Buddhist monastery at Ajanta (*see* p. 92), with its magnificent murals, or wall paintings, was built in

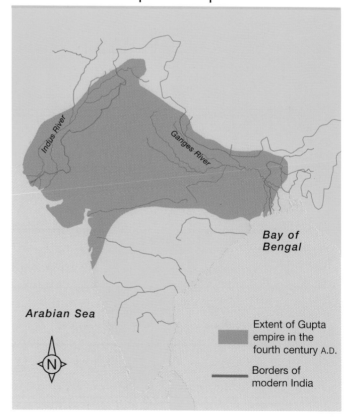

Gupta Empire

Indus River

Ganges River

Arabian Sea

Bay of Bengal

N

Extent of Gupta empire in the fourth century A.D.

Borders of modern India

the fifth century. In the field of science the astronomer Aryabhatta put forward the theory that the earth moved around the sun. We now know that this theory is correct, although it was ignored at that time. He also calculated the time it takes for the earth to revolve around the sun to 365.3586805 days, which was amazingly accurate given that there were no telescopes, computers, or calculators at the time. It was not until about 1,000 years later that the same theory was proposed in Europe, by Copernicus (A.D. 1473–1543). His theory, too, was opposed at the time. In literature, through his use of images and his choice of words, the writer Kalidasa took the Sanskrit language to new poetic heights. The Gupta age also saw the Hindu caste system become more established, as did the idea that women's position in society should be inferior to men's.

> The south of India achieved great wealth through its trade with other civilizations. These included both the Egyptians and the Romans, who bought spices, ivory, and silk from the Indians in return for gold.

By the end of the sixth century A.D., the Gupta empire had collapsed and the last great Hindu empire of the north was at an end. Smaller kingdoms tried to gain power, and groups from the northwest started to invade. The next few centuries saw different groups seize power. Among these groups were the Rajputs who, from the seventh century A.D., became a major power in northwestern India. The Rajputs of Rajasthan were a warrior race. Independent centers of Rajput power sprang up but the Rajputs were never strong enough to take overall control. The intricately carved temples of Khajuraho, in northeast India, date from the Rajput dynasty of the Chandelas (A.D. 916–1203).

The First Muslims in India

Initial incursions by Muslim Arabs into India were relatively peaceful. The Arab troops of Mohammed ibn al Qasim allowed Hindus to continue practicing their religion. This changed with the invasions of the Turkish commander Mahmud of Ghazna (Ghazna included modern Afghanistan and Iran). Between A.D. 1000 and 1027 he made 17 raids into India, looting Hindu temples, and massacring the inhabitants.

This began a period of Muslim attacks on India, from the Persian Mamluk dynasty, then came the Khaljis, and finally the Tugluqs. By the time that Tamerlane the Great's incursions into India in 1398 (see opposite) brought about the breakup of the Arabian sultanate (the empire which ruled part of India), Muslim influence had been firmly established in northern India.

MUSLIM INVADERS

Successive Muslim invaders from Central Asia swept into India—the Turks, the Afghans, and the Mongol leader Timur, or Tamerlane, plundered the northern plains. Until the arrival of the Muslim Mughals in the 16th century, and their subsequent domination of India, power shifted between Muslim invaders and the resident Hindus. The Hindus were often at a disadvantage because local rivalries stopped them from forming a unified defense. In addition, the Hindu caste system allowed only the warrior caste, the Kshatriyas, to fight in battle, thereby limiting the number of available men. Hindu foot soldiers and elephant-mounted soldiers were no match for the quicker Muslim invaders' archers on horseback. The boundaries of the successive Hindu kingdoms grew and shrank.

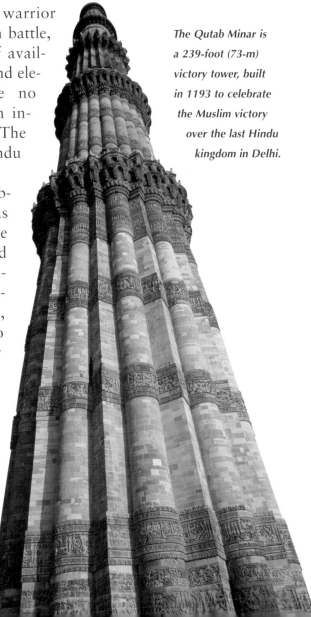

The Qutab Minar is a 239-foot (73-m) victory tower, built in 1193 to celebrate the Muslim victory over the last Hindu kingdom in Delhi.

The Delhi Sultanate was established in A.D. 1206. A sultan was a type of Muslim ruler, and the land that he controlled was called a sultanate. Whereas previous invaders had been content to compromise with the local Hindus, the latest conquerors wanted to impose the religion of Islam. By A.D. 1225 the Delhi Sultanate had all of the Ganges River basin under its control.

In southern India, the Muslims never presented a real threat. Since the eighth century, Muslim Arab merchants had traded on the western Malabar coast. They were not interested in extending

The six great Mughal emperors:
Babur
(1527–1530)
Humayun
(1530–1556)
Akbar
(1556–1605)
Jehangir
(1605–1627)
Shah Jahan
(1627–1658)
Aurangzeb
(1658–1707)

their influence beyond business, and when the Delhi Sultanate tried to extend its power south, it was repulsed.

The Delhi Sultanate lasted for 320 years and over six dynasties. The Mughal dynasty was the most successful. Today, around India and particularly Delhi, there is plenty of evidence of the cultural and artistic achievements of the Mughal empire.

The Mughal Empire

The Mughal empire represented the high point of Islamic rule in India. There were six great Mughal rulers who oversaw a golden age of building, art, and literature. At its height, under Emperor Akbar's reign (1556–1605; *see* box opposite), the Mughal empire expanded to an extent seen previously only under Asoka and later under the British. The Mughals' passion was building and they constructed some of India's greatest buildings, including one of the world's most famous, the Taj Mahal (*see* p. 99).

The founder of the Mughal empire was Babur. His reign lasted only three years, from 1527 to 1530, but he was responsible for defeating the sultan of Delhi. His grandson, Akbar, extended and consolidated the empire. Akbar was skillful in subduing the Rajputs of Rajasthan and then diplomatically

The Mughal Empire

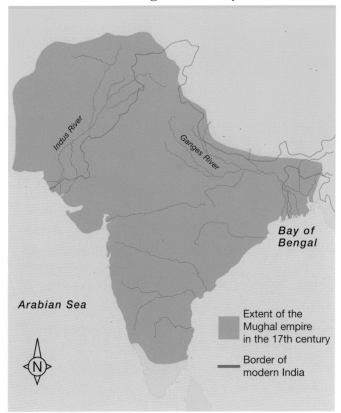

Indus River

Ganges River

Bay of Bengal

Arabian Sea

N

Extent of the Mughal empire in the 17th century

Border of modern India

Emperor Akbar

Akbar became emperor in 1556 when he was only 13. He ruled the Mughal empire until 1605. When he was only 15, Akbar conquered a large part of central India, and then went on to take control of the state of Rajasthan. In order to conquer the neighboring state of Gujarat, Akbar marched 600 miles (1,000 km) in only nine days from his newly built capital, Fatehpur Sikri, with 3,000 horsemen.

Akbar's skills were not restricted to his military prowess. He established an efficient system of government and was also a skilled diplomat. Akbar realized there were too many Hindus in India to ever convert them to Islam. Instead of treating them as second-class citizens, he married a Hindu woman and integrated the Hindus into his empire by using Hindu advisers, generals, and employing Hindus as administrators. He spoke to leaders of other religions and established religious tolerance in the empire. Although he could not read or write, Akbar promoted the arts and literature. He encouraged the development of the Mughal school of miniature painting—a skill that was introduced from Persia (modern-day Iran)—and is the central figure in the miniature painting above.

made the defeated Rajput generals into the governors of his newly conquered territories.

Akbar's son, Jehangir, took the throne after his father's death and followed his basically good and enlightened rule, although he spent little time outside the state of Kashmir. Shah Jahan, who reigned from 1627 to 1658, secured the throne by executing all his male relatives. A firm and successful administrator, and responsible for some of the marvels of Mughal architecture, Shah Jahan was eventually imprisoned by his second son, Aurangzeb, in the Agra Fort across the river from the Taj Mahal, which Shah Jahan had built, and spent his last seven years able to glimpse the distant Taj only as a reflection on a small piece of glass.

When Aurangzeb inherited the throne in 1658, the Mughal empire was becoming increasingly difficult to

A miniature of Shah Jahan ("Ruler of the Universe") and his beloved wife Mumtaz Mahal, for whom he built the white marble mausoleum, the Taj Mahal. She died giving birth to their 14th child.

rule. Intent on expanding the empire's boundaries still farther, Aurangzeb imposed heavy taxes on his subjects to pay for his military campaigns. This, combined with his obsession to make India a Muslim state, led to the empire's downfall. Revolts and rebellions broke out across the empire and these were increasingly difficult to stop. After Aurangzeb's death in 1707, the Mughal empire's fortunes declined. Although there continued to be Mughal emperors, they had no effective power.

The Maratha Empire

In the Maharashtra region of west India, nonBrahmin (nonpriestly) castes organized themselves into a formidable fighting force under their legendary leader, Shivaji. In the 18th century, the Marathas moved quickly to subdue other areas. Such was their fighting prowess that other states were soon paying them "protection money" to prevent their raids.

By 1751 the Marathas controlled enough of India that their territory could be called an empire. Sensing the weakness of the Mughals in the north, foreigners invaded the territory of the Mughals. When Afghan forces invaded Delhi in 1757, the Mughals employed the Marathas to defend their territory. In 1761 Afghan armies met the Marathas in battle. The complete defeat of the Marathas brought their imperial aspirations to an end. It was this power vacuum at the end of the 18th century that allowed the European powers who traded in India to enter into the area.

The Maratha empire controlled much of central India but failed to halt the influence of the European powers on the subcontinent.

Maratha Empire

Indus River

Ganges River

Arabian Sea

Extent of the Maratha empire in 1805.

---- Borders of modern India

THE EUROPEANS

In 1498 the Portuguese explorer Vasco da Gama (1460–1524) landed at Calicut, in the state of Kerala on the southwest coast of India. The Portuguese explorer reached Calicut by sailing around the southern tip of Africa, the Cape of Good Hope. The Portuguese were the first Europeans to set up permanent links with India. Early in the 16th century, they established a colony in the state of Goa, which they kept until 1961. They also established naval stations to the north. The Portuguese failed to make inroads into the rest of India, however, and it was other Europeans who established stronger trade links with India. European trade was very small compared to that of the Indian traders.

During the 17th century the English, French, Dutch, and Danish all set up East India companies to trade with India. They came to buy Indian textiles, dyes such as indigo, and spices. Of the Europeans who came to India, only the British and French were serious contenders for power. The Dutch concentrated on the East Indies (present-day

Spice Trade

Spices have been at the heart of Indian trade for thousands of years. India first became a trading partner with Western countries thanks to its wealth of spices. The fertile slopes of the Western Ghats produce black pepper, cardamom, cinnamon, cloves, garlic, turmeric, and nutmeg. The earliest trade was with the Sumerians, Phoenicians, Arabs, Greeks, and Romans. Traders from China, Portugal, and England followed.

Explorers such as Marco Polo, Vasco da Gama, and Christopher Columbus, set sail from Europe in search of spices, which were highly prized in Europe as flavorings in cooking. In 16th-century Europe, spices were used to mask the flavor of rotting meat. The prices of most spices exceeded that of gold by weight. Traders were able to inflate prices because they controlled the supply.

In India spices are used both in cooking and in medicines. Indians believe that spices affect behavior differently. They use spices when preparing food to produce the six tastes (rasas) of sweet, salty, bitter, astringent, sour, and pungent, considered necessary to every meal.

Europeans in 17th-century India

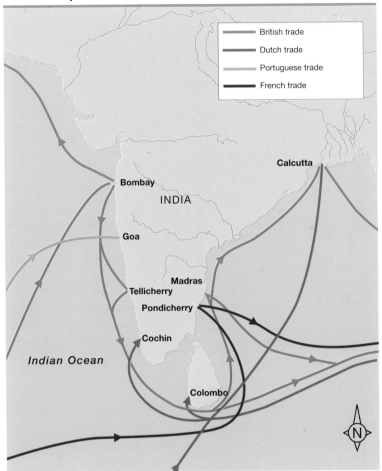

British trade
Dutch trade
Portuguese trade
French trade

Calcutta

Bombay

INDIA

Goa

Madras
Tellicherry

Pondicherry

Cochin

Indian Ocean

Colombo

N

While the French, Dutch, and Portuguese controlled specific areas of the Indian coast, the British used military force to seize the Indian possessions of other European powers.

Indonesia), the Portuguese were content in Goa, and Danish involvement was very small. As the Mughal empire broke into smaller states, the Mughal rulers could only look on as the Marathas, the French, the British, and local governors fought for control of its former lands.

The British East India Company employed small armies to protect its commercial interests. The armies were often better equipped than their Indian counterparts, with the result that several Mughal rulers sought their protection. In return for stationing troops on their territory, the Mughal rulers paid money to the company, often at a very high price.

The British East India Company was established by 80 London merchants in 1599 and had 27 trading posts in India by 1647. By the late 17th century the company had established a trading post at Fort William, which was later to become the city of Calcutta (Kolkata).

This late 18th century Mughal painting shows an official of the East India Company riding on an elephant, surrounded by his Indian servants.

BRITISH RULE

The British presence in India began with trade, but once Britain became involved in the affairs of local Indian states to protect British trade, it began extending its territory. This process continued throughout the 18th century. Successive regional powers were brought under control of the British East India Company. Gradually, British interest in India stopped being purely commercial and started to encompass all aspects of Indian life. As this slowly happened, the British government started to assume more power from the East India Company.

The British defeated their main European rivals, the French, in a series of battles. In 1746, events in India brought France and Britain to war there. The French seized the British base at Madras (Chennai), but Britain regained it in 1749. A short peace followed before the Seven Years' War between the two powers on a worldwide basis from 1756 until 1763. The British emerged as victors following the Battle of Plassey in 1757, when they defeated the *nawab* (prince) of Bengal, who was responsible for the Black Hole of Calcutta (*see* p. 38). At the time, Bengal was the richest of the Mughal provinces, and its wealth was being used by the British to finance their war against the French. In 1761, the British captured the east coast port of Pondicherry from the French, bringing the French challenge for control of India to an end.

Britain continued to expand its territory in India, but there was fierce opposition from Sikhs in the northern Punjab region, the Marathas in the west, and the Mysore sultans of the south. The Marathas were not defeated until the 1816–1818 war with the British. Their defeat owed more to internal divisions than to British military skill. By 1818 much of India was in ruins and the British set about claiming it as their own.

Under British rule, India remained no more united than it had been previously. The British oversaw 562 princely states that were supposed to be independent but in reality came under strong British influence. The princely states remained in existence until independence in 1947 when, with the exception of Kashmir, they were included in the newly created countries of India and Pakistan.

In order to bring some unity to its huge colony and to maximize trade, the British set about building an infrastructure of railroads and telegraph stations and improving roads and steamship

The Princely States

On November 1, 1858, the first viceroy of India (the representative of the British king) announced the British government's new directive on India. Abandoning their previous policy of unification of India, the British now decided to support the local "princes, chiefs, and peoples of India," resolving not to intervene in religious matters. Christian missionaries were discouraged from working in the country for fear of Hindu and Islamic revolts. The British saw the rivalry of hundreds of local Indian states as "natural breakwaters," preventing a united uprising against British economic domination. One condition of the statement was that the states and their princes must swear loyalty to the British crown. The British built military bases around the country, living separately from most Indians. The local princes were free to settle local matters, while the British dominated trade.

services. They introduced British systems of policing, law and order, and civil service. Indians were employed at low-ranking positions—they could not advance, for example, beyond a certain level in the army. On March 7, 1835, English was made the national language of India, thereby establishing British domination. Britain took over India's industries for its own profit. India's textile industry, for example, was destroyed by the compulsory import of British textiles. Resentment among Indians grew.

Divide and Rule

The British realized that India was too important to be ruled by a private company. Henceforth, India was to be ruled by the British Crown and in 1858 a representative, or viceroy, was sent to rule India on behalf of the British queen, Victoria. After the 1857 mutiny (*see* box below), the British used the lessons learned from the uprising to implement their divide and rule policy. The mutiny had

The 1857 Mutiny

Less than 50 years after the British had ousted their European rivals from India, they suffered their first major setback—a large-scale uprising called the Indian Mutiny. The precise origins of the mutiny are uncertain, but one cause was distrust of the British. A rumor spread that the British were going to introduce new cartridges for the Indian sepoys' guns. Sepoys were Indians serving in the British Army. It was rumored that the cartridges had to be waterproofed by a mixture of pig and cow fat, and the sepoys would have to bite the cartridge before loading. The cow is sacred to the Hindus, and the pig is unclean to the Muslims, so the

action would have offended almost all Indians. In May 1857, 85 sepoys were thrown into jail in Meerhut, near Delhi, for refusing to use the new cartridges. The next day a mutiny started. During the following 18 months, it spread through most of the army units across north India. Civilians joined in, but the mutiny failed because the Indians were not unified and many supported the British.

The 1857 mutiny was a key moment in India's history. It marked not only the end of the Mughal empire but also the end of the power of the British East India Company. The British government took overall control of India in 1858.

failed because of the lack of unity and trust between different groups of Indians. The British realized it would be to their advantage to keep different religious and racial groups at odds with each other. To this end, they denied Muslims opportunities for education and employment. This in turn created tension between Muslims and Hindus as the Muslims resented advantages bestowed on Hindus.

The Days of the British Raj

The British empire had extended its rule over India. The British Raj—a Hindi word meaning rule—began to turn India into a British colony in order to serve Britain's needs. In the early days of the British East India Company, male British colonists had sought to integrate themselves into the Indian way of life, whether it was by taking an Indian wife or by learning Hindi. As the British became more involved in India, new recruits from Britain made the five-month sea journey and brought

A colonial officer is waited on by Indian servants during the British Raj.

with them their wives and children. A separate society evolved. By and large, the British stopped mixing with the Indians and created in India a replica of British life thousands of miles away. They employed Indians as servants and socialized only with other Britons in their whites-only clubs.

The opening of the Suez Canal in 1869 cut the sea voyage from England to India from five months to five weeks, and more British expatriates arrived to work in the Indian Civil Service (ICS). Although the ICS was supposedly open to Indian recruits, the examinations were held in London, and only one Indian ever passed. Resentment among the Indian educated classes grew stronger.

Resistance to the Raj

In 1885 educated Indians from all over the country met in Mumbai (Bombay) to form the Indian National Congress Party. The idea for the party was born out of growing resentment toward the British. Ironically this resentment had been aided by the common use of the English language. Indians from different parts of the country who had previously been unable to communicate with each other now used English to communicate. The newly formed party was made up largely of professional Hindus who wanted to gain more involvement in the civil service. The party split into a moderate element that wanted to work with the British, and a more radical, nationalist element that wanted to preserve all things Indian.

At the start of the 20th century, India's population fell as famine and plague killed many people. The British government failed to

The National Congress

In 1885, the first Indian National Congress Party meeting had 73 representatives from every province of British India. Two were Muslims, 54 were Hindus, and the rest were Jains and Parsees. Delegates were wealthy, educated men —over half were lawyers. The Congress quickly became popular within India, despite British disdain. By 1888, the number of delegates had risen to 1,248. But not until the partition of Bengal in 1905 did the Congress achieve real concessions of power from the British.

South Asia in 1900

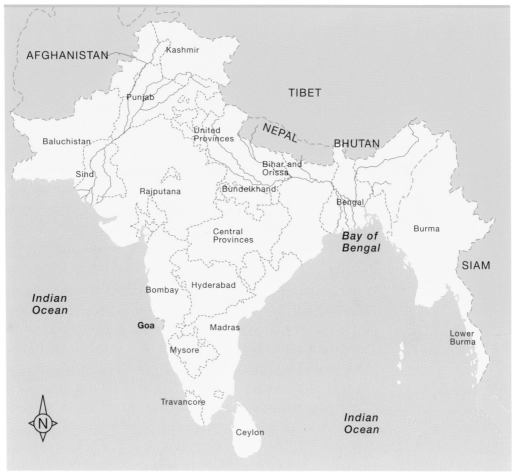

provide any improvements in living conditions. When the viceroy, Lord Curzon, made Tibet part of the British empire in 1904, Indians began to realize that the British were more interested in expanding their territory than in the welfare of the Indian people.

In 1905 the British, continuing their divide-and-rule policy, decided to partition the state of Bengal and give most of the territory to the Muslims. Outraged, the Bengalis organized a boycott of British goods, particularly textiles. The Hindu boycott marked the beginning of the end of the Raj, although the Muslims largely supported the British. To this end, the Muslims, who, at this

India became a British Crown Colony after the Mutiny of 1857. By 1900, former independent states such as Hyderabad and Rajputana had been absorbed into the British empire.

point, made up about a quarter of the population of India, founded their own political party, the All-India Muslim League, in 1906. They claimed to represent all Muslims, although many Muslims belonged to the Congress Party and challenged the claim of the League's name. The creation of two parties showed how successful the British divide and rule strategy had been.

The Moves Toward Independence

The Liberal Party in Britain won the elections of 1906 with a large majority. The British government, now under Liberal Party control, ushered in some small reforms in India. At the same time, the British used severe repression to put down India's growing demands for self-rule. In 1911, worn down by continual opposition and violence, the British revoked the partition of Bengal. The move outraged Muslims who had gained more power under the partition. When the British decided to move their capital from Calcutta (Kolkata) to Delhi the same year, Hindus were upset by the fall in real estate prices in the former capital.

Britain's promises to give India greater freedom were forgotten when the British went to war with Germany in 1914. Throughout World War I, Britain expected, and received, support from its Indian colony. About one million Indian soldiers fought for Britain. Indian troops suffered a disproportionately high casualty rate and experienced racism at the hands of their British officers. Despite this treatment, Indian soldiers were admitted to the ranks of British officers, beginning in 1917. The Indians fought willingly in the hope that Britain would grant them increased self-rule after the war in recognition of their sacrifice.

By 1918, a figure had emerged in India who was to transform the calls for self-rule into a fight for independence. Mahatma Gandhi (1869–1948) was to become the leader of the Congress Party and the architect of India's fight for independence (*see* box opposite).

India's contribution to the British war effort between 1914 and 1918 was immense. More than 1 million Indian troops were shipped overseas with 100,000 casualties and 36,000 fatalities. India also provided a huge amount of military supplies and revenue.

India. Independence became inevitable. Gandhi was vehemently opposed to the division of India into Muslim and Hindu states, but Jinnah was intent on it.

In August 1946, a year after the end of the war, Jinnah launched "Direct Action Day"—a series of peaceful rallies and demonstrations for a Muslim state. The day ended in violence with more than 4,000 dead. Riots erupted in Calcutta (Kolkata) and Hindus massacred Muslims in Bihar and Uttar Pradesh. A bloody civil war spread throughout India as Muslims fought Hindus. Britain announced it would withdraw from India in June 1948, but the continuing violence led it to decide, in June 1947, that the partition of India into two separate countries was the only way to move. In 1947, Britain decided to withdraw, bringing India independence almost one year early.

The Calcutta police use tear gas during an attempt to set fire to a Hindu temple in August 1946. Over 200 were killed in the city's disturbances alone.

INDEPENDENT INDIA

India was declared independent on August 15, 1947. Pakistan had been granted independence the previous day. At independence, Muslims made up one-fifth of the total population of India, and although they formed the majority in parts of northwestern and east India, many were scattered throughout the rest of the country. A straightforward split between a Muslim and Hindu region was impossible. Instead, Pakistan was given two regions—one to the west and one to the east (present-day Bangladesh) separated by 1,300 miles (2,000 km) of Indian territory.

It is estimated that some 13 million people were then forced to migrate between India and Pakistan. Muslim, Hindu, and Sikh openly fought each other, mainly in the partitioned states of Bengal and the Punjab. The bloodbath that followed left one million people dead

The Muslim states of East and West Pakistan were separated by a thousand miles of Indian territory. East Pakistan seceded from West Pakistan in 1971, becoming the new nation of Bangladesh.

Indian Partition 1947

and territorial claims unresolved. India and Pakistan went to war almost immediately over Kashmir (*see* p. 16). Gandhi walked through the riot-torn cities of India in an attempt to stop the killing. But he was assassinated by a Hindu fanatic in January 1948.

Jawaharlal Nehru (1889–1964) became the first prime minister of an independent India. He succeeded in putting in place a centralized, government-controlled economy. In order to bring some stability after the strife of partition, he needed to introduce a constitution that would draw all the different strands of India together and to build a strong economy. Nehru introduced three five-year plans to increase India's industrial and agricultural output. Grain production increased tremendously and investment and foreign aid followed in the early 1960s. Nehru accepted aid from both the capitalist United States and the communist Soviet Union. India's northeastern border was invaded by China in 1962 and it lost a small area of northeastern territory. In 1965 a dispute with Pakistan, which was supported by the United States, pushed India closer to the Soviet Union. After Nehru's death in 1964, his daughter Indira Gandhi (1917–1984; no relation of Mahatma Gandhi) led the Congress Party to victory in 1966 and 1971. Her socialist policies resulted in large annual increases in industrial output and a Green Revolution fueled by the introduction of high-yield grain varieties (*see* p. 79).

Muslims in India pile aboard any vehicle for Pakistan after the partitioning of India in 1947.

The official hostess for her father Jawaharlal Nehru while he was prime minister (1947–1964), Indira Gandhi took over his role two years after his death.

The Formation of Bangladesh

In East Pakistan, the brutal repression of calls for independence from the dictatorship of General Yahya Kahn had by 1971 led to a flood of refugees from East Pakistan into India. In December 1971, Indian armed forces launched simultaneous attacks on East and West Pakistan and within two weeks had totally defeated the Pakistani army. This led to the formation of the new Muslim nation of Bangladesh in the former territory of East Pakistan.

Protests at rising inflation in India and corruption within Congress in the early 1970s led to the opposition's attempts to impeach Indira Gandhi. She declared a State of Emergency in June 1975, suspending civil rights and introducing strict press censorship. The move lost her the 1977 elections in an atmosphere of protest, but the coalition led by Morarji Desai's Janata Party fell apart within two years and by 1980 Indira was back in power. Four years later she launched an ill-advised attack on Sikh protestors at the Golden Palace at Amritsar, who were demanding a separate Sikh state, Khalistan. The desecration of the Sikh's holy shrine led to the assassination of Indira Gandhi by her Sikh bodyguards in October 1984.

Indira was succeeded by her second son, Rajiv Gandhi (1944–1991), but increasing tensions at local levels and accusations of corruption led to the victory of V.P. Singh. His Janata Party, supported in coalition by the Hindu fundamentalist BJP party (*see* box opposite), lasted until late 1990. In the election campaign that followed in 1991 Rajiv Gandhi was assassinated by Sri Lankan extremists, angered by the Indian army's intervention in the Sri Lankan civil war.

Recent Developments

The Congress Party swept back to power in 1991 under P. V. Narasimha Rao, who opened up the Indian economy to foreign investment, which provided a huge boost to industry. The 1990s also saw increased tension between Muslims and Hindus erupt into violence. Hindu fundamentalist parties such as the BJP and Shiv Sena gained increasing support as the situation escalated. Once again, there were charges of corruption against the Congress Party. This and the withdrawal of key agricultural subsidies led to a disaster for the Congress Party at the 1996 elections, with the BJP becoming the largest party in Congress for the first time. It attempted to form a coalition government with several smaller parties, but this administration received a vote of no confidence in 1997, leading to new elections in March of the following year. Thirteen months later Atal Behari Vajpayee's 13-party coalition was brought down by the Congress Party. This time the Congress Party was unable to form a government and elections

The BJP Party

The Bharatiya Janata Party, or BJP, is a Hindu nationalist party, meaning that it aims to favor the concerns of the Hindu majority instead of those of other religions. The party first won popularity in the late 1980s after allegations of corruption tainted the ruling Congress Party. The BJP gained additional notoriety internationally following its support of the destruction of a mosque in Ayodhya in 1992. Claiming that the Muslim temple had been constructed on the site of a previous Hindu temple, the BJP supported the destruction of the mosque and the building of a Hindu temple. The destruction of the temple prompted an outbreak of revenge attacks in Mumbai and Delhi in 1992, but many Hindus were impressed by the BJP and joined the party.

In May 1996, the BJP came to power briefly in a coalition, but this was short-lived. Again, in 1998 the BJP emerged as the largest party but without an overall majority. A further election was called for 1999, and the BJP leader Atal Bihari Vajpayee became the new Indian prime minister of a multi-party coalition.

Prime ministers of India since independence:
- J. Nehru (1947–1964)
- G. Lal Nanda (1964; 1966)
- Lal Bahadur Shastri (1964–1966)
- I. Gandhi (1966–1977; 1980–1984)
- Morarji Desai (1977–1979)
- C. Singh (1979–1980)
- R. Gandhi (1984–1989)
- V. P. Singh (1989–1990)
- C. Shekhar (1990–1991)
- P. S. Narasimha Rao (1991–1996)
- A. T. Vajpayee (1996)
- H. D. D. Gowdah (1996–1997)
- I. K. Gujral (1997–1998)
- A. T. Vajpayee (1998–)

followed for the third time in as many years. The elections produced a coalition of right-wing parties with Vajpayee remaining as prime minister.

POLITICS AND GOVERNMENT

Since its independence India has been a federal republic. The country is split into 28 states and seven union territories. Indian national, or central, government is based on the British system. The federal government is led by the prime minister and a council of ministers, who are responsible to the two houses of parliament.

The People's Assembly (*Lok Sabha*), or lower house of the Indian parliament or Congress, has 543 members who are directly elected by the Indian people and two members who are appointed by the president. They serve a five-year term. The Council of States (*Rajya Sabha*), or upper house, has no more than 250 members, of whom up to 12 are chosen by the president. The rest are directly elected. All members serve a five-year term.

The president serves a five-year term and is elected by the two houses of parliament and members of the regional parliaments through an electoral college. The president's duties are mainly ceremonial—he or she must follow the advice of the council of ministers and the prime minister.

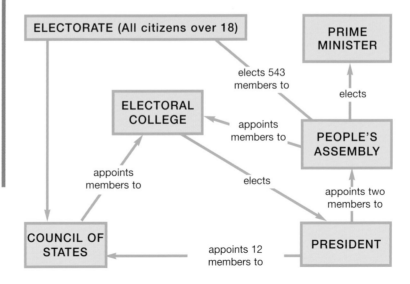

THE INDIAN PARLIAMENT TODAY

Prime Minister Atal Behari Vajpayee (since March 19, 1998)

People's Assembly (*Lok Sabha*)
545 members • Last election 1999 • Elections held every 5 years

BJP Bharatiya Janata Party	33%
Cong. (I) Indian National Congress	21%
CPI Communist Party of India (Marxist)	6%
Other	39%

Council of States (*Rajya Sabha*)
250 members • Last election 1999 • Elections held every five years

Cong. (I) Indian National Congress Party	25%
BJP Bharatiya Janata Party	18%
CPI Communist Party of India	6%
Others	51%

Indian politics is dominated by the BJP and the Congress Party. Both, however, rely on the support of smaller parties to form a government.

Each state has its own parliament. Some have two chambers like the national parliament. State governments are headed by a chief minister. If the affairs of a state are seen to be getting out of hand—as has happened in the state of Jammu and Kashmir—the federal government can intervene and impose direct rule from Delhi. Each state also has a governor appointed by the president.

Each state is responsible for health, education, forest, and transportation excluding railroads. The quality of services varies enormously—as can be seen in education. In Kerala literacy is 91 percent, while in Bihar state, it is only 62 percent.

The main national political parties are: the BJP, Congress Party, Janata Dal Party, the Communist Party of India, and the Bahujan Samaj Party, representing the caste of the Untouchables. In addition there are at least 37 state parties, and more than 300 other registered parties. Because of the high illiteracy levels in India, each political party uses a pictorial symbol. The BJP's symbol is a lotus flower; the Congress Party uses a hand; and the Janata Dal Party, a wheel.

The Economy

"India has an immense reservoir of resources and inner strength. If we tap this reservoir, the benefit will be a hundred times more than we pay."

Indian prime minister Atal Bihari Vajpayee

In 1999 India's economy was the 15th-largest in the world with a Gross National Product (GNP) of $357 billion. A country's GNP is the value of all the goods and services that country produces in a year. Although India has the world's second-largest population, its GNP is relatively small. In comparison, China, the world's most populous country, has the seventh-largest GNP, and the United States, with the world's third-largest population, has the largest GNP in the world.

The reason for India's relatively low GNP is that its economy is predominantly based on agriculture. All the world's leading economic powers are industrial nations. Industry is becoming increasingly important and India is one of the world's top ten emerging industrial nations. Following changes to the way the economy was run in 1991, India opened up its economy to foreign investment. As a result the economy grew for much of the 1990s.

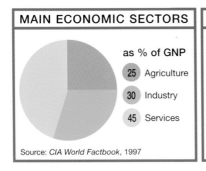

MAIN ECONOMIC SECTORS

as % of GNP

25 Agriculture
30 Industry
45 Services

Source: *CIA World Factbook*, 1997

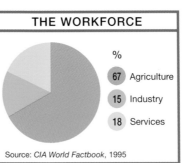

THE WORKFORCE

%

67 Agriculture
15 Industry
18 Services

Source: *CIA World Factbook*, 1995

India is the largest producer and consumer of tea in the world. The main growing areas are Assam, West Bengal, Kerala, and Tamil Nadu.

INDIA'S ECONOMY AFTER INDEPENDENCE

After Indian independence, the first prime minister, Jawaharlal Nehru, created an economy planned and controlled by the national government. In the 1950s, Nehru tried to copy the Soviet Union's planned industrial development using a series of "five-year plans" to increase industrial production through more government control. He allowed private investment and control in agriculture and other "non-essential" industrial sectors. Initially his plans were only partly successful. Three monsoons devastated Indian agriculture in the early 1950s, leading to the country's dependence on foreign aid for a few years. However, the economy picked up and a "Green Revolution" in farming in the 1960s rapidly increased farm output, leading to surpluses in the 1980s.

India is the third-largest producer of cotton in the world after China and the United States. The crop forms the basis of the country's largest export, textiles.

Planning and Foreign Aid

The Indian government's role in the economy has traditionally been extensive. So vast is the country's population and so wide the range of economic enterprises in the country—from almost medieval agricultural practices to the most sophisticated hi-tech industries—that the government has played a major role in linking different areas of the economy and attempting to plan what will be produced in order to overcome the country's huge problem of poverty.

India was dependent on foreign aid for much of the late 20th century. Its diplomatic neutrality meant that aid was received from both the United States and the Soviet Union. Initially this came in the form of food, but as India developed agriculturally, food was replaced by technological assistance and financial investment. Today India is still the third-largest recipient of international aid after China and Egypt, receiving over $1.5 billion in 1997.

A deterrent to foreign involvement in the economy was India's high taxes on imports. These taxes added to the price of goods entering the country from abroad, limited foreign involvement in the economy, and protected India's poor from the worst ravages of foreign exploitation. It also gave domestic industry the chance to develop without having to compete internationally with more efficient economies. However, in the long term, the Indian economy failed to keep up with international industrial developments and its share of international trade declined sharply in the first 40 years of independence. The lack of foreign competition proved to have as many disadvantages as advantages.

MAIN TRADING PARTNERS

EXPORTS

%
19.3 United States
6 United Kingdom
5.8 Hong Kong
5.6 Japan
63.3 Others

IMPORTS

%
9.5 United States
7.1 United Kingdom
6.8 Belgium
6.7 Germany
69.9 Others

Source: *Economist World in Figures*, 1997

India's main economic partners are with the English-speaking nations of the United States and the United Kingdom.

The Green Revolution

For a huge agricultural nation like India the introduction in the 1950s and 1960s of new chemical fertilizers, the products of Western industry, and high-yield seeds, developed by booming scientific research, was to have a revolutionary effect on rural areas. During the period of Indira Gandhi's premiership (1966–1977), the government encouraged food production by paying farmers higher prices to switch to food crops. In addition, govern-

EXPORTS ($bn)		IMPORTS ($bn)	
Textiles	8.0	Machinery and equipment	9.2
Handicrafts	6.0		
Gems and Jewelry	5.1	Crude oil and products	8.2
Engineering goods	5.0		
Chemicals	3.1	Gems	3.1
Total (including others)	34.0	Total (including others)	41.0

Source: *Economist World in Figures*, 2000

Malnutrition, a major cause of ill-health, is widespread among India's poor. Conditions in the shanty towns are made worse by a lack of basic sanitation.

ment-sponsored programs taught farmers new scientific farming methods. While India used to import food in order to feed its people, the country is now self-sufficient in food. Food distribution among India's poor, however, is another matter. India's booming industrial economy has encouraged many peasant farmers to abandon rural poverty for the hopes of a better life in the city. Unfortunately few succeed, and the vast shanty-towns that surround India's larger cities are a testament to the country's enduring problem of feeding its people—now more a problem of dividing the available food rather than any overall shortage.

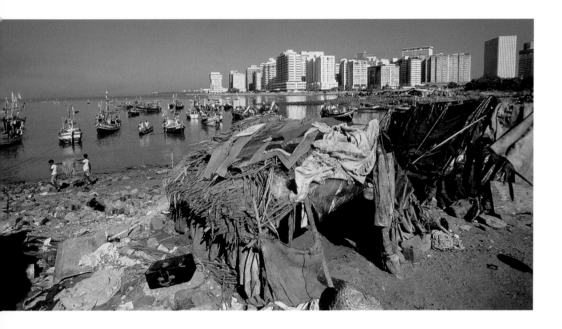

Dwellings in India's shanty towns, such as this site on Mumbai's coastline, are made of all manner of found materials.

Industrial Expansion

During the period of the Green Revolution, industrial output still lagged behind agriculture, comments by Nehru suggest that he did not believe industry to be so important in India's economy and as a result it was largely left outside of the government's control. By the 1980s, although India continued with the five-year plans—in 1998 it was halfway through the ninth plan—economic reform and a relaxing of economic controls had started to take place. The process of opening up India to foreign investment and competition was started by the then-prime minister, Indira Gandhi, in the early 1980s and was continued by her successor, her son Rajiv Gandhi. However, by the end of the decade, those who had profited under the old inefficient system put the brakes on reform, and by the early 1990s, the economy was stricken by a fall in the value of the rupee and high price rises. The then-prime minister, Narasimha Rao, deregulated the economy in 1991. This meant decreasing government control, encouraging foreign investment, and cutting government spending. By the mid-1990s, the economy was booming and millions of people were benefiting from the changes. A whole new middle class was created who could afford cars and consumer goods that previously only the richest could afford.

Today, India has a wide range of industrial production ranging from textiles to rockets. The country has great expertise in computer technology, and Bangalore has become India's "Silicon Valley" (*see* p. 86). Millions of Indians living abroad contribute to the Indian economy as nonresident investors. However, alongside the booming Indian

The introduction of the free-market economy was strongly resisted by among others the Communist Party. They argued that it would destroy India's village-based communities.

Women office workers in Mumbai walk to work. Only 29 percent of the Indian workforce is female, one of the lowest figures in the world.

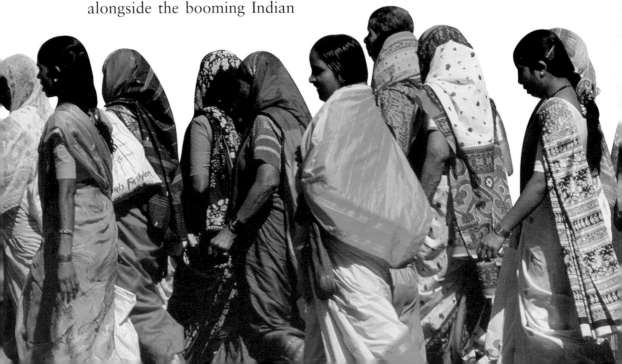

stock market, the growing middle class, and the visible levels of consumption, around half the population still lives in poverty, lacking many of the basics of life.

AGRICULTURE AND FISHING

Mahatma Gandhi said that the heart of India was in its villages. Although Indian cities are vast, sprawling places, with some of the highest population densities in the world, 75 percent of all Indians still live in rural villages. The farmers in these villages practice subsistence farming—growing just enough crops for their own consumption. They depend on the monsoon for irrigation, and when it fails, the results are devastating not only for the villages but for the economy as a whole. Sixty-seven percent of India's labor force of nearly 400 million work in agriculture, producing 30 percent of GNP.

Crop varieties and fertilizers may have changed, but most Indian farming methods still follow age-old practices.

After 1947, large farms were broken down to enable more people to own small parcels of land to support themselves. Today, more than 80 percent of India's farmland is held in units of fewer than 20 acres (8 ha).

LAND USE

Mountains
Cropland
Forest
Pastureland
Desert
Wetlands

India's large proportion of arable land and its relatively small amount of unproductive desert make the country one of the world's major agricultural nations.

More than 57 percent of India's land is cultivated for agriculture. Most farming is done in the centuries-old fashion of using manual labor and animals. A typical sight in India is of a farmer plowing his field with an ox in the shadow of an industrial plant. Terrible famines have affected India in the past, and until the 1980s, India had to import food grains. The innovative "Green Revolution" expanded irrigation of land and widened the use of fertilizer. These increased the production of food staples such as rice and wheat, and food production has doubled in the past 20 years. Since the 1980s, India has become a net exporter of rice and wheat. In addition, tea, coffee, cotton, and sugarcane are grown and contribute to export earnings. Exotic fruits such as mangos, papayas, guavas, and coconuts are grown for home use and for export.

India has a large proportion of its land under cultivation. It is fortunate in having relatively fertile soils because of flooding and silt deposits from rivers.

LAND USE

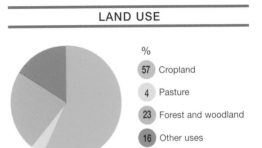

%
57 Cropland
4 Pasture
23 Forest and woodland
16 Other uses

Source: Government of India, 1997

The Fishing Industry

India has thousands of miles of coastline, and in coastal areas such as Goa and Bengal, fresh fish and shellfish are widely eaten. India ranks among the top ten of the world's fishing nations with an annual catch of 2.9 million tons (3 million tonnes). Fish such as sardines, mackerel, bummalo fish—which when dried is known as Bombay duck—and shellfish such as lobster, shrimp, crayfish, and crab are common in Indian waters. In Bengal, fish are also reared on fish farms.

The Union Carbide factory in Bhopal was the site of a poison gas leak in December 1984 that claimed thousands of lives and injured tens of thousands of the city's inhabitants.

Manufacturing Industry

Only 15 percent of India's labor force work in manufacturing industries. Nevertheless, India produces a wide range of goods such as steel, vehicles, textiles, and chemicals. Many foreign companies have factories in India because labor costs are much cheaper and health

MAJOR INDUSTRIES

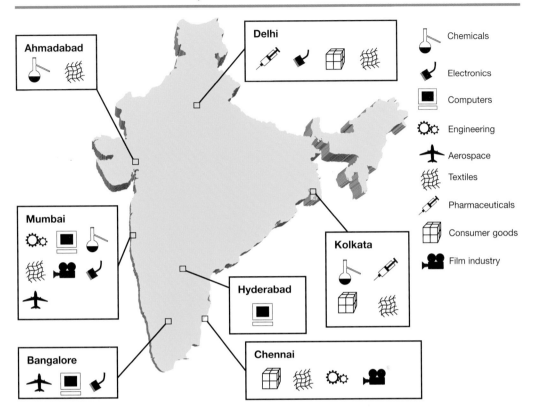

and safety regulations are not so strictly enforced. One result of this lax control was the disaster at the Union Carbide factory in Bhopal in 1984 (*see* opposite). More recently, campaigners have drawn attention to the use of child labor by Western corporations working in India.

Following economic reforms in the 1990s, industrial growth has been rapid. However, India has expanded from a small industrial base. One of the disadvantages of rapid industrialization is increased pollution. Delhi is now one of the most polluted cities in the world. In addition to heavy industry, India excels in new technology, and many information technology (IT) companies, such as Microsoft, have Indian offices. The center of the new technology is Bangalore (*see* p. 86).

Another major industry is the movie business (*see* p. 101). More than 900 new movies are made in India each

India's industry is still distributed around the old colonial centers. The production of textiles is a major industry in the villages.

Bangalore: India's Silicon Valley

Traditionally known as the garden city, Bangalore, the state capital of Karnataka, today is more often called India's "Silicon Valley." With a population of more than five million, it is one of the fastest-growing cities not only in India but also in Asia, attracting computer graduates from a wide area. The reason for its popularity among technology companies dates back to the 1960s, when the government made it the center for key defense and telecommunications research. It grew into the science and technology center of India.

Bangalore is currently home to some 200 IT companies. The largest software company, with a revenue in 1998 of $121 million, is the Indian-owned Infosys. The company's founders have set up a foundation to provide health and education for the poor. Many international companies use computer staffs based in Bangalore because labor costs in India are cheaper. The staffs are highly trained, and the time difference allows companies to operate for longer periods during the working day.

International IT companies employ highly educated graduates who enjoy Bangalore's cosmopolitan city life with its bars, nightclubs, and shopping malls, which attract tourism and bring foreign revenues into the country. The downside to the city's expansion is an infrastructure that cannot cope. Water shortages, power cuts, poor roads, and inadequate housing are everyday problems.

year, exceeding Hollywood's output. The biggest revenue earner is the "Bollywood" movie business based in Mumbai. South India has its own movie industry, producing movies in the main Dravidian languages of Kannada, Malayalam, Tamil, and Telugu. There are 12,000 movie theaters across India, and with millions of illiterate people among the population, visual entertainment is very popular. Indian movies are one of the most popular forms of entertainment.

Mineral Resources and Energy

India is rich in many natural resources such as iron ore and bauxite. There are large deposits of coal that are expected to last for the next 100 years. Along with oil and gas deposits found off the Gujarat coast, hydro and nuclear power, firewood, and even cow dung provide

ENERGY SOURCES

%

80 Fossil fuels

18 Hydroelectric power

2 Nuclear power

Source: *CIA World Factbook*, 1996

India's power. Where people do not have access to electricity, they use firewood, and the smell of burning wood at nightfall is common in cities and villages alike.

India is a major producer of gold, and everybody aspires to own gold, usually in the form of jewelry. Historically India has been an important producer of gemstones. Gems and jewelry remain the country's third-largest export.

Communications and Transportation

India's international airline is the government-owned Air India which has daily flights to the rest of the world. To fly from the East Coast of the United States to India's capital, Delhi, takes approximately 17 hours. The government-owned Indian Airlines is the largest domestic air carrier, and it competes with an ever-increasing number of private airlines to fly passengers across the country. Major airports are at Mumbai, Kolkata, Chennai, and Delhi.

While flying is the fastest way of covering large distances across India, the most popular way to travel is by the government-operated Indian Railways, which carries ten million passengers every day and is the fourth-largest railroad company in the world. It is also the world's largest employer with more than 1.6

TRANSPORTATION

— Major highways
╫╫╫ Railroad
✈ Major airport
— Navigable river

Chandigarh

DELHI
Jaipur Kanpur Lucknow
Patna Guwahati
Ahmadabad
Indore Varanasi
Surat Jabalpur
Mumbai Kolkata
Nagpur
Solapur
Visakhapatnam
Hyderabad
Goa Vijayawada
Bangalore
Mangalore Chennai
Cochin
Madurai

India has a large transportation infrastructure, as one would expect for a country of its size. Many of the country's roads and railroads are outdated, making travel between different parts of the country slow if inexpensive. As industry grows, the country will need to update its system if it is to compete internationally.

In India's remote areas, narrow-gauge railroads (those with very closely spaced rails) are the norm. These provide a bumpier journey than the city-to-city express services.

million employees. Indian trains are slow compared to the trains in the United States and Europe but they are cheaper and offer a splendid way to see the country. Different-speed trains operate all over India from the fast-link super-express Rajdhani Express, that runs between Delhi and Mumbai, to the very slow local trains. On long journeys, people turn the train into a temporary home—chatting, playing games, eating, drinking, and sleeping to while away the hours. At each of the train's many stops, food sellers jump on the train to sell their homemade food. Subsidized fares means that travel is affordable for most Indians, although some-times people travel on the train roof in order to avoid paying the fare.

Indian roads outside of the major cities are often poorly maintained. Automobile ownership is low at only four autos per thousand people (the U.S. has 489 per 1,000 people), so the impact of private vehicles is slight. However, out of a total of 1.2 million miles (2 million km) of highway, only half is paved. All types of vehicles compete for space on the roads, and on remote routes it is not unusual to see a truck or bus overtaking an elephant. Drivers have to swerve to avoid hitting cows walking along or even sitting on the road. In the cities, as more and more people own cars, it is often much quicker to walk than drive. Many people travel by bus, which operate all across India. Buses are a cheap but decrepit and often very crowded means of transportation.

Tourism

India has always attracted visitors to see its varied landscapes and historical treasures, although not as many as might be thought. In 1998 there were only 2.3 million tourist arrivals, compared with France's 70 million. In addition, India attracts backpacking tourists rather than the luxury end of the tourist market. Indian politicians have realized that tourism generates ready income and creates jobs, so they raised the budget for India's Tourism Department by $15 million to $40 million for the 1999–2000 financial year. While the Taj Mahal (*see* p. 99) is the top tourist attraction for visitors to India, the Indian Tourist Department wants to promote India's 15 other World Heritage sites in addition to the countless monuments and lesser-known parts of the country. It is eager to improve roads, rail, and air links to key tourist sites.

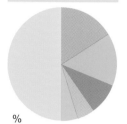

MAIN TOURIST ARRIVALS

%
16 United Kingdom
15 Bangladesh
9 United States
5 Sri Lanka
5 Germany
50 Other

Source: Government of India, 1995

An elephant ride is a must on any tourist's trip to India.

Arts and Living

"If there is a paradise on the face of the earth.
It is this, oh it is this, oh it is this."

Inscription on the Red Fort, Delhi

India's ancient and great civilization has a rich cultural tradition that has been shared with the whole world. English, an Indo-European language, owes its origin to the ancient Sanskrit language of India, devised by the Aryans. The *Mahabharata*, which is one of India's oldest texts, was the first book known to be written in Sanskrit.

Modern Indian literature is just as likely to be written in English, a legacy of the British, as in any one of India's many languages. Indian-born writers such as Salman Rushdie (born 1947), Vikram Seth (born 1952), and R. K. Narayan (born 1906) are world renowned. At the other end of the spectrum, India's movie industry is not only the world's largest but also constantly changing to meet the demands of its vast audiences.

The quality of daily life in India depends on how much money a person earns. Nevertheless, for those with money food is plentiful and cheap, and there is a wide variation between regional dishes. Roadside food vendors are a common sight in the cities. Primary-school education is free and compulsory, but high school and universities charge fees, which means that often only the children of middle-class and rich families can afford them. The growth of the IT industry in Bangalore has attracted highly educated graduates from all over India, who previously would have had to emigrate to the United States or Europe to further their careers.

One of the chief means of preserving the caste system is the "arranged marriage," where families choose a bride or groom for their son or daughter.

FACT FILE

- India's culture is one of the oldest in the world.

- The *Mahabharata* is one of the world's oldest stories.

- Cricket is India's most popular sport. The sport was introduced during the colonial period.

- The ancient Indian language of Sanskrit is one of the world's oldest languages.

- India's movie industry is the largest in the world.

- Indians living in other parts of the world and wishing to find a partner from a similar social position will often place advertisements in India hoping to find a suitable partner.

The paintings in the Ajanta caves in northern Maharashtra state are masterpieces of Buddhist art. They date from around 200 B.C. to A.D. 650.

THE ARTS

India has a long artistic tradition that dates back thousands of years, and sophisticated examples of painting and sculpture can be found all over the country. The most distinctive buildings in India were built during the time of the Mughal emperors, which was a high point in Indian architecture. The British brought with them their own building styles, and many examples of Victorian buildings can be found in India's cities. Dance and music are an important part of life in India, and every region has its own songs and dances.

Literature

Ancient Sanskrit was the first-known language of India. Its literature influenced all of ancient India's political, religious, and social life. Before a written language developed, Sanskrit poems and hymns were memorized and recited. Historians are still unable to date accurately the earliest Sanskrit hymns. The most influential Sanskrit scripts, the Vedas (*see* p. 46), deal with politics, economics, religion, and medicine and probably reached their final form only around the sixth century B.C.—although they originated much earlier. They are still read today. For example, a type of medicine called ayurvedic (*see* p. 105)—which is still practiced in India today and is increasingly popular in the West—is discussed in the Vedas. When the Vedas were written down in Sanskrit, they became the first compositions in an Indo-European language.

The *Upanishads* date from between the seventh and fifth centuries B.C. They contain the two great classics of Sanskrit literature, the epic Indian poems the *Mahabharata* and the *Ramayana* (*see* box p. 94). The latter was written by the poet Valmiki, who had a deep influence on the religious and cultural life of India. Both epic poems continue to be Hindu Indians' most loved stories. The *Mahabharata*, a poem of more than 220,000 lines, recounts the battle between the forces of good and evil represented by the Pandavas, who are the heroes, and the Kauravas, the devils. When the *Mahabharata* was made into a television series that ran for many weeks, all of India came to a standstill as illiterate villagers and sophisticated Delhi residents alike were glued to the television set. *The Bhagavad Gita*—the Hindu holy book—is an episode from the *Mahabharata*.

These boys from Imphal in Manipur state in northeastern India are portraying the Pandava brothers from the Indian epic the Mahabharata. *The brothers eventually triumph over their adversaries, the evil Kauravas.*

The *Ramayana*

The *Ramayana* tells the story of good versus evil in an epic poem that is widely seen to be South Asia's first literary poem. It tells how the god Rama was banished from his father's kingdom and leaves the city with his wife, Sita, and his helper, Hanuman, the monkey god (Hanuman crouches next to Sita in the illustration shown here). The evil Sri Lankan King Ravana kidnapped Sita. Supported by an army of monkeys led by Hanuman, Rama defeated Ravana and rescued Sita. Rama emerged from the victory as the embodiment of the perfect man (*Parushottama*). He is a perfect son, brother, and king, and the poem concentrates on his kindness and compassion. Like the *Mahabharata*, the *Ramayana* was made into a television series that attracted a huge audience who loved the dramatic battle between good and evil.

Until the 18th century, Persian was the language of the princely courts in India, and classical Persian literature was the dominant influence. Although he could not read or write, the emperor Akbar (*see* p. 53) was the greatest champion of literature of all the Mughal emperors. During the colonial period, English became the dominant language of the rich and well educated. As the use of English spread, Indians who previously had not been able to understand each other's language were able to communicate. Today this use of English has helped many Indian writers reach an international audience, and discuss ideas with one another in a common language.

India has many internationally renowned writers whose work is read far beyond India. One of the most popular is R.K. Narayan, who set his novels and short stories in the imaginary south Indian town of Malgudi. Malgudi is full of eccentric characters, and Narayan, writing in English, entertains the reader with details of the town's daily life. Modern writers such as Salman Rushdie, Vikram Seth, and Arundhati Roy (born 1961) are better known in the United States than in India. They, too, write in English. Indian writers are engaged in a heated debate. Some think Indian literature should be written in one of India's native languages, while others believe English is the best language to use because it alerts the English-speaking world to the quality of India's writers.

Rabindranath Tagore

Despite being educated in England, Rabindranath Tagore (1861–1941) wrote in his native Bengali language. Tagore was the author of numerous novels, essays, plays, and of India's national anthem, but he considered himself a poet. In 1913 he was the first Indian writer to win the Nobel Prize for Literature. Prime Minister Nehru, also a published author, wrote of Tagore: "Tagore and Gandhi have undoubtedly been the two outstanding and dominating figures in the first half of the 20th century…[Tagore's] influence over the mind of India, and especially of successive rising generations, has been tremendous. Not Bengali only, the language in which he himself wrote, but all the modern languages of India have been molded partly by his writings."

The Kiss (from *Kadi O Komal* 1886)

Lips' language to lips' ears.
Two drinking each other's heart,
*   it seems.*
Two roving loves who have left home,
*   pilgrims to the confluence of lips.*
Two waves rise by the law of love to
*   break and die on two sets of lips.*
Two wild desires craving each other
*   meet at last at the body's limits.*
Love's writing a song in dainty letters,
*   layers of kiss-calligraphy on lips.*
Plucking flowers from two sets of lips
*   perhaps to thread them into a chain*
*   later.*
This sweet union of lips is the red
*   marriage bed of a pair of smiles.*

Art and Architecture

India's humid climate has had a profound influence upon its architecture. Few early buildings survive because so many of them were made of wood.

India's ancient art and architecture was created for a religious purpose. The Buddhists, Hindus, and Muslims all created their own art. The first stone monuments were built in Emperor Asoka's reign in the third century B.C., and decorated pillars such as the Asokan pillar at Sarnath survive today. Little of the Buddhist art that flourished throughout India survives, and much of the early Hindu architecture was destroyed by the invading Muslim armies.

India's painting, sculpture, and architecture are unique because they show a consistency of style over thousands of years. Surviving ancient cave paintings and sculptures have much in common with more recent art. The historian D. D. Kosambi made the point: "For no other country is the peculiar survival and expansion of prehistory...so clearly discernible [noticeable]. This is the special historical and social character of India."

The Kailash Temple is Ellora's masterpiece. Started in the eighth century, it was hewn from a single block of stone and took over one hundred years to complete.

The murals, or wall paintings, and sculptures in the caves at Ajanta and Ellora, in west India, are the finest examples of ancient Indian art. The Ajanta murals date from as early as 300 B.C. They tell the story of the Buddha's life

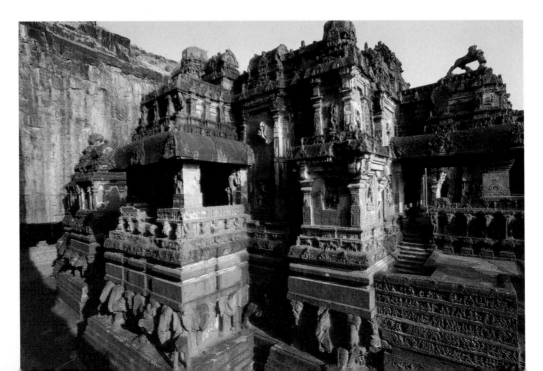

and the life and culture of the people of the time. The later Ellora caves are outstanding sculptures that were hewn out of a long cliff that stretches over a distance of some 1.5 miles (3 km). Carved more than 1,000 years ago, they depict Hindu and Buddhist religious themes. These delicate stone carvings took centuries to complete. In one cave, the Kailash Temple was carved from a single vast piece of rock. It took 7,000 stone cutters more than 100 years to complete the Kailash Temple (*see* opposite).

Indian Pottery

The art of pottery is connected both with India's most ancient myths and with the daily life of modern Indians. Brahma, the creator in the Hindu religion is often called *prajapati*, the potter, and is believed to have made the first man and woman from clay, who then gave birth to a line of potters. In India today terracotta is still largely used for containers as it keeps liquids cool. Potters also create small figurines which are used in places of worship, and potters may even intercede between the gods and the worshiper. At the harvest festival of Pongal it is customary to smash all the pots in the household and replace them with new ones.

Sophisticated sculpture is found throughout India. In Khajuraho, in east India, is a group of Hindu temples built over 100 years between A.D. 950 and 1050 during the Chandela dynasty (*see* p. 50). Famous for their erotic carvings, the temples are magnificent examples of intricate stonework that depict life in all its richness 1,000 years ago. In Mahabalipuram, on the coast south of Chennai, is a huge stone frieze, or wall decoration, that dates from the fifth century A.D. Called *Bhagiratha's Penance*, or *Descent of the Ganges*, the detailed carved frieze measures some 95 feet (29 m) long and almost 23 feet (7 m) high.

Little survives of India's ancient architecture. Some Hindu religious buildings, dating from the sixth century B.C., are still standing in south and east India. The most distinctive architecture to have survived into the modern day belongs to the much later Mughal empire. When the Muslims invaded, they destroyed most of the temples and stripped jewels from buildings. Muslims built their mosques out of the temple stone and used the jewels for their own buildings. The great period of Islamic architecture in India fused Islamic design with traditional Indian designs. Mughal emperors used local craftsmen and builders to carry out their designs. The pinnacle of this fusion was the Taj Mahal (*see* opposite).

European Influence

The Europeans in India showed little interest in mixing European architectural traditions with Indian ones. The Portuguese built several churches in Goa that look as though they have been transplanted from Portugal to India. The British left their mark on India's cities. Mumbai (Bombay), Kolkata (Calcutta), and Chennai (Madras). All have examples of British Victorian architecture in railroad stations, churches, and administrative buildings that made no concession to their being in India. Mumbai even had its own double-decker (two-level) red buses, which are still in use today, modeled on the London buses.

When the British moved their capital from Kolkata to New Delhi in 1911, they built the new capital to reflect their domination over India. It was designed by British architects, Edwin Lutyens and Herbert Baker from 1921 to 1929. They did not want to include any Indian architectural details. Opposition, however, forced the British architects to compromise and include some Indian details, although these were largely superficial additions to the classical buildings.

After India's independence, Indian architects tried to break away from colonial influence but were unsure of the direction they wanted their new buildings to take. The government commissioned foreign architects to design new buildings, such as the Swiss-born Le Corbusier (1887– 1965), who designed the city of Chandigarh.

The Chatrapathi Shivaji Terminus (or Victoria Terminal) in Mumbai was built by the British in 1887. It is a bizarre medley of the European styles that were popular in Victorian Britain.

The Taj Mahal

Recognized around the world as the ultimate symbol of love, the Taj Mahal is actually a tomb. It was built by the Mughal Emperor Shah Jahan to commemorate his wife, Mumtaz Mahal, when she died in childbirth (*see* p. 54).

The Taj Mahal marks the highpoint of Mughal architecture. Started in 1631, the tomb was built in white marble that was carried by 1,000 elephants from Rajasthan some 185 miles (300 km) away. Intricate floral patterns made out of precious stones from all over the world decorate the marble. Twenty thousand workers took 17 years to construct the mausoleum, which was not completed until 1648.

According to legend, Shah Jahan planned to build a black marble tomb for himself. He never did. His tomb lies beside that of his wife inside the Taj Mahal, where it is visited by millions of tourists each year. Today, conservationists are worried about the future of the Taj because increased pollution from nearby factories and vehicle emissions are destroying the marble. Strict rules are now in force for local industries, and polluting vehicles are not allowed within 1 mile (1.6 km) of the building.

Ravi Shankar

Born in Varanasi in 1920, the classical sitar player Ravi Shankar has been described by the Beatles' George Harrison as the "godfather of world music." Shankar first came to prominence in the early 1960s through his collaborations with the violinist Yehudi Menuhin. His influence was heard on the Beatles' 1965 song "Norwegian Wood." But his own work reached a worldwide audience with performances at the Monterey Pop Festival in 1967, at Woodstock in 1969, and at the Concert for Bangladesh in 1971. Shankar has written for opera, dance, and film. He has won two Emmys, and is an Honorary Member of the American Academy of Arts.

Indian music always has a constant drone sound, which is a reference for the audience and among the players. It is often played on a *surmandal,* an instrument like a zither.

Dance and Music

Many Indian occasions call for dance and music: weddings, births, religious processions, harvest time, welcoming a guest, and going to a new house are just some of the events that are celebrated with two of India's oldest art forms. Indians believe that sincere practice of the arts leads to the highest spiritual experience. Indian music and dance reflect the joy of life. Each Indian village has its own music and dances.

Indian dance varies from region to region. Classical Indian dance is generally divided into two types: *tandav,* which is associated with strength and masculinity, and *lasya,* which is more delicate and considered more feminine. There are four main schools of classical dance, *Bharata Natyam,* which is *lasya*; *Kathak,* which combines Muslim and Hindu influences and is both *lasya* and *tandav*; *Kathakali,* which originated in the 17th century, is usually based on stories from the epics and is danced by men; *Kuchipudi* is a dance also created in the 17th century and generally danced by men. In addition to the classical dances there are a huge range of folk dances performed at local level, many of them based on local stories and traditions.

Indian music is deeply religious. The sitar was invented in the 13th century. It is a stringed instrument and has six or seven main strings, four of which are played for melody, while the other two or three provide a drone or rhythm. Other instruments include the *subahar,* a type of bass sitar, the *sarod,* which is smaller, and an oboelike instrument called the *shehnai.* The tabla is a set of two small drums, played with the hands. Musical performances are often intimate affairs with the audience sitting on the floor close to the musician.

The Movies

The main center of Indian movie-making is Mumbai, home of the *masala* movie, which is also known as Bollywood. *Masala* means mix, and a masala movie contains a little bit of everything—romance, action, singing, and dancing. This type of movie is a "feel-good" movie: the bad guy always gets found out, and the good guy always gets his girl. The movies are usually at least two hours long because, besides the main plot, there are always subplots that all have to be resolved by the end. Only 5 percent of movies made are big box-office hits. To maximize the chances of a hit, film directors use India's most famous movie stars whenever they can. This means that popular actors may work on many different movies at the same time. One of India's most popular actors, Shashi Kapoor, was once signed up for 140 movies at one time.

The movie industry based in Chennai (below)—with 36 permanent sets, Asia's largest—caters to the southern Indian languages, while movies made in Mumbai are in Hindi.

One former actress Jayalalitha Jayaram capitalized on her popularity by going into politics in the state of Tamil Nadu, where she was briefly chief minister.

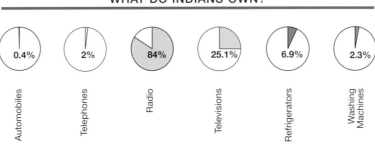

WHAT DO INDIANS OWN?

| 0.4% | 2% | 84% | 25.1% | 6.9% | 2.3% |
| Automobiles | Telephones | Radio | Televisions | Refrigerators | Washing Machines |

Source: Encyclopedia Britannica

Basic nutrition remains the priority for the vast majority of Indians.

HOW INDIANS SPEND THEIR MONEY

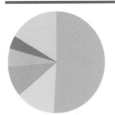

%
- 50.9 Food and drink
- 13 Transportation
- 9.8 Housing
- 5.7 Clothing
- 4.2 Health
- 16.4 Recreation/culture

Source: Encyclopedia Britannica

Another movie industry exists in India that is very different from those in Chennai and Mumbai. Disillusioned with the commercialism of the *masala* movies, a breakaway group of filmmakers created India's New Wave cinema, determined to show the reality of India. The most famous director of the New Wave was Satyajit Ray (1921–1992), who was awarded an honorary Academy Award just before he died. Movies such as *Pather Panchali* (*The Song of the Road*) brought not only Ray but also India to the attention of the world's movie-goers.

The Media

In a country in which almost half the population is illiterate, television plays a very important role in the media. Even the poorest village has at least one television set. The national channel, Doordarshan, broadcasts in both national and regional languages. Television has become increasingly popular since the introduction of satellite television in the 1980s. Satellite television has opened up the Western world to Indians, and many Indians prefer to watch Star TV, CNN, or the BBC, instead of Doordarshan.

Newspapers and magazines, written in English and India's national and regional languages, are very popular. The best-known daily English-language newspapers are the *Times of India* and the *Indian Express*. English-language magazines such as *India Today* are also widely read.

EVERYDAY LIFE

Daily life in India depends on how much money a person has. For the poorest third of the nation, each day is a struggle to feed the family. The poor live from day to day because they do not have enough money to plan for the future. At the other end of the spectrum, the rich live extremely comfortable lives, looked after by many servants. In between is the growing middle class, which increasingly looks to Europe and the United States for its role models.

Sports and Leisure

There is one sport that dominates India's sporting calendar—cricket, which was once described as "polite baseball." Brought to India by the British, cricket is a national obsession, especially in Mumbai. The game is played with two teams of 11 players on a pitch (field) 22 yards (20 m) long with a wicket (three stumps of wood) at each end. The object of the game is to score more runs

In every village and city, boys play cricket on any piece of empty land, using whatever they can as equipment. They all dream of being a top professional player.

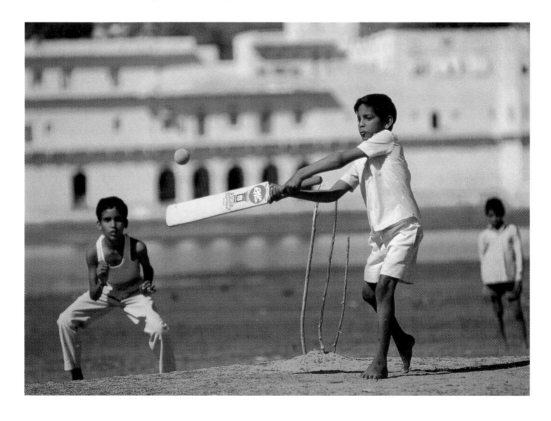

Kabadi

Kabadi is a version of playing tag and is the most played game in India. Its popularity stems from the fact that it does not require any equipment, there are very few rules, and anybody can play. Two teams of any number can play, though seven is the norm. Each team stands on either side of a central line. One person crosses to the other team's side and the object of the game is to stop him or her from getting back to their own half of the field. The opposing team chases the person, and if it catches and "tags" them, they are out of the game. The team with the most players left wins.

than the opposition. The batsman hits the ball and makes a run while the opposition team is fielding the ball, attempting to hit the stumps with the ball before the batsman can reach them. There are different types of cricket matches, lasting from one to five days. Whenever the Indian team is playing, crowds will gather around any store that has a television, and people carry little radios so they can keep up to date with the latest score. India has one of the world's best cricket teams and won the World Cup, which is held every four years, in 1983. Matches against Pakistan are the most keenly fought with an intense rivalry between the two teams. Other games played in India include soccer, field hockey—India's men's team has won the Olympic gold medal eight times—tennis, and polo, which is played on horseback.

Health and Welfare

In India health and welfare depend on two things—where a person lives and how much money he or she earns. Rich city dwellers enjoy the best medical treatment, while poor villagers may have no doctor for miles.

Each Indian state is responsible for its own health care, and is headed by a surgeon general. People usually have to pay for health care in India, but there is some provision for free medical care. Most small towns have a government-run hospital that can treat common diseases such as diarrhea and malaria. There are also some charitable hospitals in the big cities that charge fees according to how much a person earns. A person's income determines the class of hospital bed he or she gets.

In cities, doctors operate private clinics and every consultation must be paid for. Private medical insurance does not exist across India, although it is starting to appear in the larger cities. In Mumbai, for example, many private companies take out medical insurance policies for their employees.

In India at the beginning of the 21st century, many people still die from hygiene-related illnesses, such as typhoid. In an effort to prevent this, health workers now visit remote villages to teach local people the importance of clean water, sewerage, and drainage. Health workers also try to educate villagers about birth control.

Life expectancy in India varies according to how much a person earns. In 1998 men were expected to live to 61.9 years and women 63.1 years. Women have an average of 3.11 children, and India's population continues to grow at about 17 million people a year.

The reasons for this growing population are many, but one primary cause is the high infant mortality rate at 65 deaths per 1,000 children born (compared with 7 in the United States). This encourages those Indians who live in poverty to have many children in order to ensure that they have enough family members to farm the land and care for their parents in old age.

Ayurvedic medicine

The ancient *Vedas* (*see* p. 46) contain numerous references to disorders and their treatment. Ayurvedic medicine, which is based on the teachings of the *Vedas*, is an entire medical system. It aims to prevent disease by maintaining in the body the balance of the five elements of space, air, fire, water, and earth. This is done through a variety of practices, including meditation, yoga, herbal remedies, and diet. The five elements are grouped into three *doshas*—*vata* (space and air), *pitta* (fire and water), and *kapha* (water and earth)—fundamental biological energies that regulate an individual's life processes. Historically, ayurvedism was important because it marked the movement of Indian medicine away from medical practice based on superstition and toward medicine based on physical observation of the individual's symptoms. During the period A.D. 100 to 500, Indian medicine was far more advanced than that in the West. There existed a detailed knowledge of human anatomy and surgical techniques, with simple operations to remove kidney stones and cataracts being performed.

Education

Primary school education in India is compulsory. There are currently 573,000 grade schools out of a total of 820,000 schools. Grade-school education is free. In the countryside, lessons are sometimes taught under the shade of a tree because a schoolhouse is too expensive to build.

Junior high school and high school education is not free. Parents must pay for schoolbooks and tuition. Most schools insist that pupils wear a school uniform, which must also be paid for. At this level, education is not compulsory, although the government is attempting to make it so. At present, the quality of junior high and high school education depends on the state. In Kerala state, which has a communist state government, a high premium is placed on education and almost all Keralans (91 percent) are literate. In contrast, in Rajasthan in the northwest the literacy rate is only 62 percent.

Teachers are well respected in India. People look up to the guru (teacher) because of his or her knowledge. Discipline in Indian schools is not usually a problem as most children are very eager to learn.

Adult Literacy

The lack of education of many Indians is an ongoing problem for the Indian government. It has launched literacy campaigns to teach people to read and write, but with limited success. Operation Blackboard was launched in 1987 to bring literacy to 100 million adults aged between 15 and 35. Ten years later it had failed because of lack of money. India's literacy rate now stands at 52 percent, although among women this falls to 37.7%.

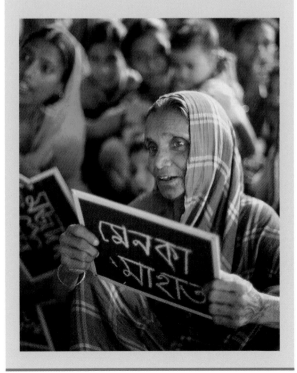

Child Labor

Often a poor family's immediate need to feed itself every day means that all the children must go out to work instead of going to school. Illiterate parents often do not understand the benefit in extra salaries an education could bring their children. Instead, they send the children onto the streets to sell gum, trinkets, or polish shoes—anything that might earn a few rupees.

In 1986 the government acted to make it illegal to employ children under the age of 14 in hazardous industries. Nevertheless, hundreds of thousands of poor and uneducated children continue to work in India today. For example, it is estimated that the carpet-weaving industry illegally employs 300,000 children. Children are employed because their small hands are able to weave the intricate patterns. They work very long days in bad conditions with poor light, few breaks, and for very little money.

There is also a problem in that Western companies working in India have been less than scrupulous about checking the real age of employees in their factories, arguing that this is the responsibility of local government. This is particularly the case in the textile and garment industries producing goods for the Western markets.

University education is not free, and usually only middle-class or rich students can afford to go. The standard of further education is very high in India, and many students go on to postgraduate work both in India and overseas. Medicine, law, and information technology (IT) are the most popular subjects for students. Many medical students leave India for successful careers as doctors and surgeons in the United States and Europe. Similarly, many computer graduates emigrated to California's Silicon Valley to further their careers, although now many are returning to Bangalore's Silicon Valley to help boost India's highly successful IT business (*see* p. 86).

Despite the low proportion of Indians attending university, higher education has expanded tremendously since independence. The number of universities has increased sevenfold. There are rigorous tests for entry to university but the number of students enrolling has increased by fifteen times.

EDUCATIONAL ATTENDANCE

Further (university) 7%

Secondary (high school) 49%

Primary 100%

How to say...

Here are a few words of Hindi, India's national language, using the English alphabet. The words would normally be written in a different script, so the suggested pronunciation here is only approximate.

Hello/goodbye *Namaste*

How are you? *Aap kaiseh hein?*

OK *Acha*

Yes *Han*

No *Nahin*

Please *Mehabarni seh*

Thank you *Dhanyavaad/shukriyaa*

Don't worry *Koi baat nahin*

Sorry *Kshamaa kijiyeh*

You're welcome *Aaap ka swagat hai*

Do you speak English? *Kya aap Angreji bolte hai?*

I don't understand *Meri Samajh men nahin aaya*

What is your name? *Aapka shubh naam kya hai?*

My name is *Meraa naam...hai*

One *Ek*

Two *Do*

Three *Tin*

Four *Char*

Five *Panch*

Six *Chhe*

Seven *Saat*

Eight *Aath*

Nine *Nau*

Ten *Das*

Sunday *Ravivaar*

Monday *Somvaar*

Tuesday *Mangalvaar*

Wednesday *Budhvaar*

Thursday *Guruvaar*

Friday *Sukhravaar*

Saturday *Shanivaar*

National Holidays and Festivals

India has very few officially recognized national holidays, but it does have hundreds of different festivals, celebrated at various times across the country. Some of India's festivals are linked to the changing seasons, such as *Vasant Panchami* in February, when people mark the arrival of spring (*Vasant*) by wearing yellow clothes. Others celebrate religious dates such as the *Buddha Jayanti*, the first night of the full moon in either April or May that marks the birth of Buddha. *Diwali*, or the festival of lights, is celebrated in October or November, particularly in north India, and is the happiest of Indian festivals. Indians believe it is important to celebrate the festival properly to encourage the gods to return to earth. Rows of lamps or candles are lit in remembrance and *rangoli*s (chalk designs) are painted on the floor as a sign of welcome. Fireworks are a key part of the celebrations, and people start to set them off days before the actual *Diwali* celebration takes place.

The most colorful of all Indian festivals is Holi. Celebrated the day after the full moon in early March, it marks the climax of spring. Processions with music, singing, and dancing take place around Hindu temples. People light bonfires on the night before *Holi* to symbolize the end of winter and the destruction of the devil Holika. But the most fun takes place on the day of *Holi* itself when it is traditional to throw colored pigment (*gulal*) and colored water at anybody. No one objects. People wear their oldest clothes since the colors can stain, and for days after *Holi*, people walk around with the telltale signs of having been hit.

National Holidays

January 26   Republic Day
(celebrates the declaration of
the republic in 1950)
August 15   Independence Day
October 2   *Ghandi Jayanti*
(Mahatma Gandhi's Birthday)
December 25   Christmas Day

Revelers cover each other in brightly colored pigment to celebrate the spring festival of Holi.

Food and Drink

In a country as large as India and with such a diverse climate, it is not surprising that food varies from region to region. In north India and in the largely Muslim areas, the daily diet consists of meat, vegetables, and Indian breads such as *naan* and *chapati* (*see* opposite). In strict Hindu families in the state of Gujarat, most people are vegetarian. In the south, fish is a staple in coastal areas, and rice is a more important part of the diet than in the north. South India is also home to the *thali*, a complete meal of vegetables, rice, Indian bread, and even dessert served on the same plate.

A woman sells fresh puris (crispy, puffed-up, deep-fried bread) at her stand on the streets of Hampi in central southern India.

Usually every meal is freshly prepared, which means cooks spend a lot of time in the kitchen. There are staples that appear at every meal such as rice, Indian breads, and dhal. *Dhal* is a thick stew usually made with dried lentils. It is very nutritious, and it is said there are as many variations of *dhal* as there are families in India.

India has its own "fast food." Street vendors sell popular snacks such as *bhelpuri*. *Bhelpuri* is made of thin, crispy lentil-flour noodles, puffed rice, and wheat crackers mixed with diced boiled potatoes, chopped raw onion, coriander, and different chutneys. It is the most popular snack in Mumbai, and street vendors have their own secret blends of ingredients. *Bhelpuri* is best eaten immediately, while everything is crispy.

India makes its own versions of soft drinks with names such as Thums Up!. Indian drinks include freshly squeezed tropical fruit juices that can be bought from roadside vendors. A very refreshing drink is fresh coconut water, which is available everywhere in the south. Roadside vendors cut fresh green coconuts open with a machete. The coconut milk is then drunk through a straw. When the customer has finished drinking, the vendor scrapes out the soft coconut flesh for the customer to eat. Lassi is a drink made of yogurt thinned with water and with either salt or sugar added according to taste. Served with ice and a sprinkle of fresh cardamom spice, it is very refreshing on hot days. Hot tea, flavored with spices and boiled with milk and sugar, is an extremely popular drink at any time of the year.

Many Indian desserts are milk-based. Some of the most popular are *kulfi*, an Indian version of ice cream flavored with cardamom, pistachio nuts, and saffron; *gulab jamun*, which are spongy ground almond balls, deep fried and then soaked in a saffron syrup and eaten cold; and *firnee*, a rice and milk dessert served with almonds, raisins, and pistachios. For those who prefer something lighter there is fresh fruit such as mangoes, bananas, melons, tangerines, guavas, pomegranates, and pineapples.

Chapatis

Chapatis are to India what *tortillas* are to Mexico. They are very easy to prepare: Mix wheat flour with water until the mixture can be rolled into a ball. Break off a little of the mixture and roll it into a thin circle. Heat up a skillet but do not add any fat. When the skillet is hot, put the *chapati* in and cook until it starts to puff up. Turn it over and cook the other side in the same way. Remove the chapati from the skillet and serve while still warm. *Chapatis* can be served with any meal or as a snack with Indian chutneys or a salsa of diced tomato, onion, coriander, and a squeeze of lemon.

RELIGIOUS LIFE

India is a secular state, meaning that it has no official religion. Nevertheless, it is a deeply religious and spiritual country. Following independence and the partition of India, the country is now predominantly Hindu. Eighty percent of Indians are Hindu, 14 percent Muslim, 2.4 percent Christian, 2 percent Sikh, and Buddhism now accounts for only 0.7 percent. The rest of the population are Jains or belong to other religions. Hinduism and Buddhism, along with Jainism, which has approximately five million followers, are some of the world's oldest religions. Buddhism and Jainism were both started as a reaction to the rigid rules of Hinduism.

There is great cross-fertliization between Christianity and Hinduism. In the state of Tamil Nadu Christians do not eat beef or pork. In many places Indian Christian women wear *tilak* dots on their foreheads.

Islam

Although Muslims comprise only a small percentage of the population, there are more than 100 million Muslims in India, making it one of the largest Islamic populations in the world. Islam is a relatively young religion. It dates from the seventh century A.D. when the religion's founder, the prophet Mohammed (A.D. 570–632), received revelations, or visions, from Allah (God). Mohammed's visions were written down and collected in what became Islam's holy book, the Koran. Muslims believe that the one God, Allah, who created the world, is all powerful and wise, and will one day bring the world into final judgment.

The sixth-largest mosque in India, the Mecca Mosque in Hyderabad was built in 1598. Its central arch contains red bricks from Mecca.

The Muslim holy day is Friday, and the main mosque (temple) in every city is known as the Friday mosque. Every male Muslim has to pray five times a day by facing toward Mecca in Saudi Arabia, Islam's holiest city. Once a year, every Muslim has to fast from sunrise to sunset for the month of Ramadan, and every Muslim must try to make a pilgrimage to Mecca.

Hinduism

Hinduism is the largest religion in Asia with more than 700 million followers in India alone. Hinduism is unusual in relation to other world religions in that it has no founder or prophet, and no central text or creed. Instead Hinduism has evolved over many centuries, absorbing influences from other religions. As a result its beliefs can seem complex and contradictory to outsiders. A person can only be born into Hinduism and, unlike most other world religions, one cannot convert to Hinduism. At birth, every Hindu belongs to a caste that he or she cannot leave (*see* p. 114). The castes determine the social standing within the Hindu community. At the top of the caste system are the Brahmins, or priests. Next is the warrior caste, the *Kshatriyas*, who are either soldiers or administrators. Then the *Vaishyas*, who make up the artisan or

Hindu Gods

Hinduism has many gods, of which the trinity of Brahma, Vishnu, and Siva are the most important. Brahma is the creator; Vishnu is the preserver and sustainer. His incarnations are Rama and Krishna, the preserver. Siva is both creator and destroyer. Other gods are worshiped for different reasons. In Bengal, Kali, the goddess of destruction, has always been worshiped, and in Mumbai, Lakshmi, the goddess of wealth, is a favorite. Two very popular gods that are seen all over India in temples and homes are the animal gods Ganesh, the elephant god, and Hanuman, the monkey god.

The Caste System

The four castes are said to come from different parts of the creator Brahma's body: the Brahmins from his mouth, the *Kshatriyas* from his arms, the *Vaishyas* from his thighs, and the *Shudras* from his feet. Beneath all these castes are the Untouchables, or *Dalits*. Their job is to perform tasks considered demeaning, including the cremation of the dead. Being born into one caste does not necessarily determine a person's occupation. For example, many Brahmin caste members are poor farmers. An Indian street cleaner, however, will almost always be a member of the *Dalits*. Discrimination against the *Dalits* was made illegal in 1947, but it still persists today. In an attempt to improve conditions for the *Dalits*, the government reserves a large number of public sector jobs and university places for this caste alone.

commercial class, followed by the *Shudras*, who are the farmers and peasant class.

Hindus believe that life is eternal and consists of a series of births that can be ended only by reaching spiritual salvation (*moksha*). Each reincarnation either leads closer or farther away from salvation depending on karma, the law of good and bad causes. Good actions in life mean a step closer to stopping the rebirth cycle; bad actions mean further reincarnations. There are three basic religious practices in Hinduism: daily prayer (*puja*), cremation of the dead, and the laws and practices of the caste system.

The beliefs of Hinduism were collected together in a set of texts called the Vedas (*see* p. 46) between 1000 B.C. and A.D. 500, although they had been transmitted orally for many centuries prior to this. Later Hindu texts include the *Brahmanas*, which deal with sacrifice, and the *Aranyakas* or "forest treatises."

Founded in Persia (modern Iran) in the sixth century B.C., Zoroastrianism involves worship of the god Ahur Mazda, who is symbolized by fire. In India followers are known as Parsees (because they originally came from Persia) and mostly live in Mumbai.

Buddhism

For several centuries Buddhism dominated the religious life of India. Although it originated in India and is still a major religion in other parts of Asia—notably parts of China and Japan—today Buddhism is largely confined to northeast India, although many important Buddhist monuments still exist throughout the country. Buddhism was founded in (around) 560 B.C. by Siddharta Gautama, known as the Buddha, a princely Hindu who had been born in present-day Nepal. Disenchanted with Hinduism, the Buddha formulated the concept of *dharma*, the true nature of the world and the teaching that there is no self. The only way to achieve the peaceful state of nirvana is to accept that everything in the material world is impermanent and subject to change. Nirvana is achieved by an eightfold path characterized by the renunciation of the material world and the search for a true understanding of human experience.

Sikhism

The Sikh religion is dominant in the Punjab, located in northwest India. It shares elements with Hinduism and Islam but has a distinct identity from both. Sikhism's founder was Guru Nanak (1469–1539), who regarded the many gods of Hinduism as names of one supreme God. He preached that all people have the possibility of escaping the cycle of death and rebirth regardless of caste by becoming centered on God. Guru Nanak's teachings were further expounded by nine succeeding gurus during the centuries after his death.

Jainism

Jainism is based upon the teachings of Mahariva, who was active in the sixth century B.C. Like Buddhism it seeks escape from the endless cycle of rebirth, and this is achieved by following a path of austere living, meditation, care for all living things, and rejection of impure action. The Jain population of about five million is today largely concentrated in the state of Gujarat in the northwest of India.

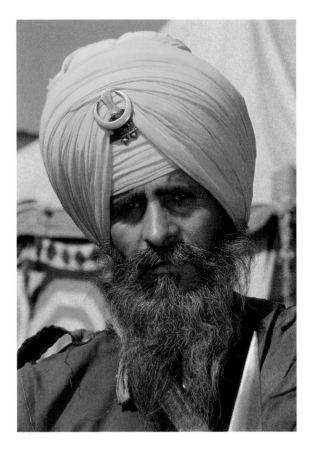

The Sikh brotherhood of khalsa *is represented by five emblems:* kesh *(unshorn hair);* kangha *(a comb);* kaach *(short trousers);* kirpan *(a sword);* kara *(a steel bracelet, representing the link with God).*

The Future

"India has the sanction of her own past glory and future vision to become strong—in every sense of the word."

Indian prime minister Atal Bihari Vajpayee

On the face of it, it might seem that India, as it starts the 21st century, is beset with problems. Its ever-growing population, the 1999 war with Pakistan over Kashmir, the rise of Hindu fundamentalism, and regional demands for independence all suggest that India has a troubled future. However, thousands of years of experience have taught Indians many valuable lessons that should help them deal with, if not solve, their difficulties.

The most obvious problem facing India is its increasing population. By 2030 it will have overtaken China as the world's most populous nation. As the population grows, increasing pressure is put on India's infrastructure, such as its railroads, roads, and schools. Jobs, housing, and food all become more difficult to find for everybody. India's forests are disappearing as people destroy natural habitats for food, fuel, and housing.

India's relationship with Pakistan is another immediate concern. In 1999 the war between the two countries at Kargil, in Kashmir, and both countries' nuclear weapons testing saw relations worsen. During the 1990s, the Bharatiya Janata Party capitalized on anti-Muslim feeling and encouraged the rise of Hindu fundamentalism. This has led to some persecution of other religious minorities. Elsewhere across India—such as in the Punjab and in the south—people have agitated for independence, and the threat of localized conflict is never far away.

Many in India hope that small-scale industry will fire other areas of the economy and allow the country to capitalize on its vast workforce.

FACT FILE

- By 2003, India's software industry will be the country's biggest foreign currency earner.

- Less that 11 percent of India is still forested.

- India tested nuclear weapons in 1998 and 1999.

- Mumbai, Delhi, Kolkata, and Chennai are all among the world's top 30 most populated cities.

- The cost of living in India is one of the lowest in the world, third-lowest behind Libya and Zimbabwe.

- India currently has 16 percent of the world's population living on 2.4 percent of the world's landmass.

Socially, India has changed rapidly in the last 15 years of the 20th century largely because of the increased influence of the West. Foreign programs on television and the ability of more people to travel overseas were two major influences on Indian life. Today, particularly in middle-class families, there is a struggle between the traditional Indian values and Western materialism and consumerism.

REASONS FOR OPTIMISM?

Despite the problems, there are reasons to think that India's future will be bright. Although the population continues to rise, Indian women are having fewer children. The chief reason for the continuing population rise is that Indians are living longer as hygiene and medical care improve. Despite having so many mouths to feed, India is self-sufficient in food production. In 1998 food grain production hit a record 200 million tons.

In the 1999 elections, the BJP downplayed its anti-Muslim and pro-Hindu attitude, emphasizing instead its pledge to open up more of the economy to private investors. The party recognized that it would gain more political success from promoting the economy than from stirring up religious differences. India's economy

Ecological Issues

India's developing economy presents new problems for the country's ecology. Deforestation is a major problem, and less than 11 percent of India's dense forests remain. Local nature reserves may often fail to get the protection they require because of the corruption of local politicians. Delhi and Mumbai are among the most polluted cities on earth and levels of carbon monoxide in Delhi can reach as high as 50 times the recommended levels of the World Health Organization. The problem is compounded by the use of old and inefficient machines and automobiles.

In comparison to the United States or Western Europe, however, national levels of pollution are low. While the rate of increase is alarming, it will take India at least 20 years before the country's emissions of carbon dioxide begin to approach those of the United States.

is, of course, crucial to the country's future. The seeds for growth have been sown—in 1999 the stock market hit record highs, inflation was very low, and the economy grew. With such a huge domestic market, India is seen by many in the West as a potential economic superpower.

Despite the fact that almost half the country cannot read or write, India has one of the world's best university systems. It produces a huge number of postgraduate students, and most university courses are taught in English. High levels of knowledge and the use of the English language have helped bring about India's information technology (IT) revolution. In 1998 total software exports totalled $2.6 billion, despite the fact that the market is still in its infancy. Indians possess the knowledge and technical capability to progress far into the IT market. It is hoped that a trickle-down effect will occur—that is, that the growth of the industry will create jobs for Indians all over the country, not just in the IT centers. Despite the importance of the IT industry, India only had 100,000 internet connections in 1998, a tiny figure considering the population of the country. A major problem in India is the unreliability of the national telephone system. As a result of this problem, the government set aside $300 million to invest in updating the country's telecommunications system.

The key to India's future lies in its people and their huge capacity for hard work and study. India's vast workforce make it an obvious player in the world economy, and the cost of paying this workforce remains so low that India is able to undercut many of its economic rivals. The growth of domestic industry means that while skilled Indians used to move to the United States to further their career, they are now able to stay in India to achieve the same goal. Their presence should help the less well-off and less educated in their home country. Taxes that they pay will go to the Indian government rather than to the U.S. government and their greater spending power should boost the Indian economy further.

In 1998 the United States imposed sanctions against India for its testing of nuclear weapons and for escalating the arms race with Pakistan. The sanctions appeared to put a brake on international investment at that time.

Almanac

POLITICAL

Country name:
Official long form: Republic of India
Short form: India
Local form: *Bharat*

Nationality:
noun: Indian(s)
adjective: Indian

Official language: Hindi and 16
other official languages,
including English

Capital city: Delhi

Type of government: federal republic

Suffrage (voting rights): everyone 18
years and over

National anthem: "*Jana Gana
Mana*" ("Thou art the ruler")

National holiday: January 26
(Anniversary of Proclamation
of the Republic)

Flag:

GEOGRAPHICAL

Location: Southern Asia; latitudes
8° to 37° north and longitudes
68° to 98° east

Climate: Temperate in north, tropical
monsoon in south

Total area: 2,042,870 square miles
(3,287,590 sq. km)
land: 90%
water: 10%

Coastline: 4,350 miles (7,000 km)

Terrain: mountains in north, desert in
west, flat plains in east, upland
plain in south (Deccan Plateau).

Highest point: Mount Kangchenjunga,
28,169 feet (8,586 m)
Lowest point: Coastline on the Indian
Ocean, 0 feet (0 m)

Natural resources: coal, iron ore,
manganese, mica bauxite,
titanium ore, chromite,
natural gas, diamonds,
petroleum, limestone

Land use (1993 est.):
arable land: 56%

forests and woodland: 23%
permanent pastures: 4%
permanent crops: 1%
other: 16%

Literacy:
total population: 52%
male: 65.5%
female: 37.7%

POPULATION

Population: 1.014 billion

Population density: 496 people per square mile (308 per sq. km)

Population growth rate (2000 est.): 1.58%

Birthrate (2000 est.): 24.79 births per 1,000 of the population

Death rate (2000 est.): 8.88 deaths per 1,000 of the population

Sex ratio (1999 est.): 107 males per 100 females

Total fertility rate (2000 est.): 3.11 children born for every woman in the population

Infant mortality rate (2000 est.): 64.9 deaths per 1,000 live births

Life expectancy at birth (1999 est.):
total population: 62.5 years
male: 61.89 years
female: 63.13 years

ECONOMY

Currency: Indian rupee (Re);
1 Re = 100 paise
Exchange rate (2000):
$1 = 43.55 rupees

Gross national product (1999):
$357 billion (15th-largest economy in the world)

Average annual growth rate (1990–1997): 6%

GNP per capita (1999 est.): $370

Average annual inflation rate (1990–1997): 9.8%

Unemployment rate : widespread unemployment

Exports (1997): $34 billion
Imports (1997): $41 billion

Foreign aid recieved (1996): $1.68 billion

Human Development Index
(an index scaled from 0 to 100 combining statistics indicating adult literacy, years of schooling, life expectancy, and income levels):
45.1 (U.S. 94.2)

TIME LINE—INDIA

World History

Indian History

c. 50,000 B.C.

c. 40,000 Modern humans—*Homo sapiens sapiens*—emerge.

c. 2,000–1200 B.C. Period of Minoan, Hittite, and Mycaenean, Mediterranean expansion.

c. 753 B.C. Rome founded.

c. 2500 B.C. Harappa civilization flourishes on banks of Indus River.

c. 2300–2000 B.C. Harappa civilization trades with ancient Sumeria.

c. 1500 B.C. Aryans begin to move south through India.

c. 1500–1200 B.C. Vedic scriptures written.

c. 500 B.C.

499–494 B.C. Revolt of Ionian cities against Persian rule leads to rise of Classical Greece.

c. 500 B.C. Emergence of Buddhism in India.

326 B.C. Alexander the Great reaches India but does not conquer the region.

c. 1350–1550 Italian Renaissance leads to rebirth of the arts and classical learning in Europe.

c. 1000 Vikings reach American continent but do not settle.

c. 632–1530 Period of Islamic expansion in Middle East, Europe, and North Africa.

476 Fall of Rome to the Goths.

c. A.D. 1 Birth of Christ

c. 112 B.C. Chinese open Silk Route in the east.

146 B.C. Fall of Carthage begins Mediterranean expansion of Roman empire.

1398 Tamerlane the Great makes raids on India.

1206 Delhi Sultanate established.

c. 1000 Mahmud of Ghazna begins raids on India.

c. 1000

Eighth century Muslim traders establish bases on west coast.

Seventh century Rajputs a major power in northwest India.

A.D. 320 Gupta empire founded.

A.D. 0

190 B.C. Bactrian Greeks begin 400 years of foreign invasions in India.

232 B.C. Death of Emperor Asoka.

321–184 B.C. Period of Mauryan empire.

350 B.C.

c. 1500

1492 Columbus lands in America.

1520 Birth of Protestantism—the Pope expels Martin Luther from the Catholic church.

1620 First African slaves brought to America.

1498 Vasco da Gama lands at Calicut.

1527 Babur founds Mughal empire.

1605 Death of Akbar.

c. 1700 Decline of Mughals and rise of Maratha empire.

2000 The West celebrates the Millennium—2,000 years since the birth of Christ.

1989 Communism collapses in Eastern Europe.

1999 Indian nuclear tests.

1998 BJP comes to power.

1991 Rajiv Gandhi assassinated.

1984 Assassination of Indira Gandhi.

1975 State of Emergency.

1971 Secession of Bangladesh.

1966 Indira Gandhi becomes prime minister.

1962 China invades India.

1948 Gandhi assassinated.

1947 Independence and Partition of India.

c. 1750

c. 1750 Industrial Revolution begins in England.

1776 American Declaration of Independence.

1789 French Revolution begins.

1914 World War I begins.

1917 Revolution in Russia leads to establishment of Soviet Union.

1918 World War I ends.

1756–1763 Seven Years War between Britain and France for control of India.

1857 Indian mutiny against British rule.

1858 British government announces policy of support for princely states.

1885 First Indian National Congress meets in Delhi.

1905 Partition of Bengal.

1919 Amritsar massacre.

1969 First man lands on the moon.

1963–1975 Vietnam War.

1957 Foundation of the European Economic Community (EEC).

1947

1945 End of World War II, defeat of Germany.

1939 World War II begins.

1929 Wall Street Crash, beginning of Great Depression.

1946 Muslim League's Direct Action Day.

1937 Congress Party wins spectacular victory in elections.

1930 Gandhi's Salt March.

1920

Glossary

ashram: A Hindu center for religious learning and spiritual practice.
ayurvedic: Referring to a system of medicine based on the Vedic scriptures.

Brahmin: A member of the highest, priestly caste.

capitalism: An economic system based on supply and demand, and private ownership of businesses and industry.
caste: A person's social level, determined by their birth.
coalition: An alliance of one or more political parties, usually to form a government.
communism: A social and political system based on a planned economy in which goods and land are owned by everyone and in which there is no private property.
constitution: A written collection of a country's laws, its citizens' rights, and beliefs.

dharma (**Hindi**): Sense of religious and social duties in Hinduism and the path of truth in Buddhism.

export: A product that is sold to another country.
European Union (EU): An organization made up of European countries that work together on many economic, social, and political issues.

foothills: Lands sloping toward the base of a mountain range.
fundamentalism: Strict adherence to the basic beliefs of a religion, usually involving the exclusion of other belief systems.

ghats (**Hindi**): River banks.

Harappan: Referring to the earliest known civilization in India *c.* 2500 B.C.
Hindi: The most widely spoken of India's 17 national languages.
Hinduism: The historic religion of India, based on a large number of gods and originating in the second millennium B.C. (*see* p. 113).

import: A product that is bought from another country.
industrial: Describing an economy based on developed industries and infrastructure rather than on agriculture.
Islam: Religion founded in Arabia in the seventh century based on obedience to Allah.
IT: Information technology.

karma: The balance between good and bad actions, determining a person's status or caste at rebirth.

Lok Sabha: The lower house of the Indian parliament.

maharaja: Indian king.
maidan: Open green space.

manufacturing: The process of turning simple, basic materials into complex goods.
masala: Literally means "mix", a type of Indian movie that includes various different types of narrative.
masjid: Mosque.
monsoon: A period of intense rainfall occurring in India between June and October.
mosque: A Muslim place of worship.
multinational: A company or corporation having divisions in more than one country.
mural: A wall painting.
Muslim: A follower of the teachings of Islam.

nationalization: The taking of private companies or corporations into public ownership.
nirvana: State of peaceful happiness and freedom from rebirth in Buddhism.

open market: A market without tariffs (a charge imposed by government to limit certain types of trade) or other trade barriers.

partition: The separation of pre-1947 India into the three separate areas of India and East and West Pakistan.

Raj: Literally means "rule," the period of British rule in India, lasting from the 18th century until 1947.

Rajya Sabha: The upper house of the Indian parliament.

republic: A government in which the citizens of a country hold supreme power and where all the citizens of the country are equal under the law.

sadhu: Hindu holy man.

sanctions: The withdrawal of trade or other economic provision in protest at a particular political action. Usually enacted by one country upon another.

Sanskrit: The ancient language of India.

Sikhism: Religion founded in the 16th century based on the teachings of Guru Nanak (*see* p. 115)

sitar: A long-necked string instrument that is played by plucking.

shanty: A ramshackle dwelling made from found materials, usually on the edges of a large town.

socialism: Economic and political system founded on public or state ownership of the means of production.

tabla: A set of two small drums played with the hands.

the West: The countries of Western Europe and North America.

Vedic: Referring to the *Vedas*, a series of ancient religious texts, which were composed between 1500 and 1200 B.C.

Bibliography

Major Sources Used for This Book

Craven, Ros. *Indian Art*. London: Thames and Hudson, 1998.

French, Patrick. *Liberty or Death*. London: Flamingo, 1994.

Spear, Percival. *History of India Volume II*. London: Penguin, 1992.

Thapar, Romila. *History of India Volume I*. London: Penguin, 1994.

General Further Reading

Encyclopedia of World Cultures. ed. Lynda A. Bennett; Boston: G.K. Hall & Co., 1992.

The Kingfisher History Encyclopedia. New York: Kingfisher, 1999.

Student Atlas. New York: Dorling Kindersley, 1998.

The World Book Encyclopedia. Chicago: Scott Fetzer Company, 1999.

Further Reading About India

Brown, Dale M (ed.). *Ancient India: Land of Mystery*. New York: Time Life, 1995

Cawthorne, Nigel. *The Art of India*. New York, Laurel Glen, 1997.

Rai, Raghu (ed.). *A Day in the Life of India*. San Francisco: Collins Pub.; 1996.

Some Websites About India

www.indiaembassy.org (Indian Embassy in Washington, D.C.)

www.nic.in/stat (Indian Government Office of Statistics)

www.welcometoindia.com/home.html

http://w3meadev.gov.in/culture/overview.htm

www.britannica.com (type in "India" in the Search field)

www.mrdowling.com/612india.html

www.pbs.org/edens/anamalai

www.angelfire.com/in/myindia/tajmahal.html

http://rubens.anu.edu.au/student.projects/tajmahal/home.html

www.victorianmemorial-cal.org

Index

Acknowledgments

Cover Photo Credits
Corbis: Charles Lenars. (Taj Mahal); **AKG, London: Nou, Jean-Louis** (Asoka Pillar); **Tony Stone: Manoj Shah** (crouching tiger)

Photo Credits
AKG London: Nou, Jean-Louis 44, 48, 54, 72 **Colin Tilley Loughrey:** 18, 20, 76, 88,110 **Corbis:** Dave Bartruff 89, Betteman 67, 68, 71, Burnstein Collection 92, Stephanie Colasanti 30, Peter Guttman 99, Lindsay Hebberd 93, 109, Robert Holmes 40, Jeremy Homer 51, Hulton-Deutsch Collection 65, Catherine Karnow 32, 81, 101, 106, Earl & Nazima Kowall 38, 115, Charles & Josetta Lenars 19, 21

Chris Lisle 12, Philadelphia Museum 94, Richard Powers 103, Chris Rainer 84, Dave Samuel Robbins 15, Galen Rowell 90, Francesco Venturi / Kea Publishing Services 37, Staffan Widstrand 28, Adam Woolfitt 96 **Hulton Getty:** 69 **Hutchison:** Carluz Freire 112, Goycoolea 66, John Hatt 29, Julie Mighet 1, 34, C. Pemberton 33 **Peter Newark's Military Pictures:** 53 **Robert Hunt Library:** 61 **Still Pictures:** 116 **Tony Stone:** Glen Allison 6, Anthony Cassidy 78, Chris Haigh 98, Adrian Murrell 80, Manoj Shah 26 **Tony Tilley:** 82 **Werner Forman Archive:** Victoria & Albert Museum 58, De Young Museum, San Francisco 113